ADVANCE PRAISE

"What an amazing story! This book is so inspiring, motivational, and full of great leadership management tips."

—Renetta Quintana
Regional VP, Capstone Real Estate Services, Inc.

"Jerry Banks presents real-life experiences and advice to succeed and realize your dreams. From business to politics to family life, he shows you how to reset your inner GPS and manage the roller coaster of life. Leading candidate for best book title of 2024!"

—Brent Siegrist
Iowa State Representative

"Jerry shares life with poignant anecdotes and emotive integrity. This is a must read for those considering their own journey with resiliency."

—Bryce Wells
CEO, RFG Logistics

"Practical, easy to understand, and a true philosophy for all who take advantage of Jerry Banks' success. A beautifully told story, with love, life, friendship, and tragedy. I highly recommend you read this book!"

—Karie Pein
RN

"*Eat Sh*t & Smile* is a delightfully entertaining and, at times, poignant look at the ups and downs of a life well lived with some great midwesterner advice for life and business. It's a must-read for everyone both young . . . and not so young."

—Karen Sauer
Broker, Luxury Real Estate Consultant, Scottsdale, AZ

"In *Eat Sh*t & Smile*, Jerry Banks looks back, battle-worn but happy, at a life and career he built for himself and his family. Part memoir and part self-help, this brutally honest American story hits on familiar yet unique themes—love, loss, struggle, bitterness, success. It testifies to the epic story that resides in each of us and the lessons we can pass along."

—Sal Recchi
Award-winning newspaper and magazine editor, retired

"The lessons in this book are brought to life with the sometimes funny and sometimes sad, real depictions of muddling through life. It shows us that life ain't always perfect and sometimes you have to eat shit and smile.'"

—Janet Slusky
Interior Designer

"Reading *Eat Sh*t & Smile* is akin to having a conversation with Jerry Banks. He has a refreshingly honest way of sharing his life stories and imparting his experience and wisdom to the reader. I highly recommend this book to anyone from early professionals seeking guidance to seasoned veterans needing a reminder of how they got there."

—Danel Jung
EVP, COO, Dakota REIT

"Jerry's writing style is lively and continually interesting. Particularly his use of enjoyable, well-remembered stories that bring his experiences to life. His writing reveals many insights to a life well lived that has meaning to others."

—Jerry Slusky
Attorney at Law

"Jerry's book is a must-read for anyone seeking wisdom on how to achieve peak happiness and great joy throughout life. He educates the reader on how to explore bold dreams and maintain a positive mindset to achieve them. *Eat Sh*t & Smile* offers a window into Jerry's journey and how he created happiness and success in his varied endeavors."

—Matt Pedersen
President & CEO, Dakota REIT

"This revealing book is a must-read for anyone who has, or will, face significant life challenges, and, of course, we will all face significant life challenges. Jerry Banks presents a rational analytical framework for addressing the highly emotional issue of defeating life's difficulties."

—Gary M. Gotsdiner
Chairman, McGill, Gotsdiner, Workman & Lepp, PC, LLO, law firm

"*Eat Shit & Smile* provides a reflection on Jerry's life experiences, both business and personal, sharing wisdom and lessons learned on the path to success. Sprinkled with humor, wit, and charm, Jerry's stories keep you engaged throughout. I couldn't put it down!"

—Amy Thompson
CPA, partner at Rossitto & Associates

"Through years of experience and deep introspection, Jerry developed a commonsense guide to getting the most out of life. His template for decision-making can help young people avoid many of life's curveballs by properly assessing situations and making choices consistent with achieving their goals. Truly a remarkable life story."

—Roy Schumacher
Operating Partner at Dominus Capital

"Life is hard and at times unfair. Jerry believes we all have an internal GPS that will guide us to our desired destination, but only when we give our GPS the correct inputs. He explains steps to access our internal GPS and trust our intuition through his life stories, examples, and what he calls the 4D's +1. This book is inspiring, captivating, and a must read."

—Mark Boyer
Real Estate Investor

"I must be honest and admit that the title gave me pause, but when I dove in, I found an amazing story of a man who overcame trials and setbacks with determination and vision. Jerry Banks pulls no punches when it comes to his failures, showing in transparent detail how he learned from those moments and grew as a person and leader."

—Dave Burchett
Four-time Emmy Award-winning sports television director for Olympic, Major League Baseball, and NCAA football and basketball broadcasts

"*Eat Sh*t & Smile* exceeded my expectations with its engaging narrative and insightful exploration of overcoming life's challenges. Jerry's story, marked by hardships and trials, is a testament to resilience and determination in achieving success in both career and personal life. I highly recommend this book to anyone looking for inspiration and practical advice on overcoming obstacles and seizing opportunities."

—Mark Doll
Doll Distributing

"I couldn't put down *Eat Shit & Smile* from the moment I started reading. Jerry pours vulnerability into each page. By weaving personal and professional growth stories with life's setbacks, Jerry has written a must-read book for anyone at any stage of their life or career."

—Lesley Brandt
Co-Founder, Planit Inc.

EAT SH*T & SMILE

EAT

SURVIVING AND THRIVING ON THE ROLLER COASTER OF LIFE

SH*T &
SMILE

JERRY G. BANKS

Peacock Proud
PRESS

Editors
Laura L. Bush, PhD, peacockproud.com
James Thole

Cover Design
Erin Napoli, blushcactus.com

Interior Design
Medlar Publishing Solutions Pvt Ltd., India

Portrait Photographer
Cindy Maurer, csphotographystudio.com

*This book is dedicated to
my daughters Kelley and Lindsay.*

TABLE OF CONTENTS

FOREWORD

Jerry and I met shortly after I moved to Omaha in 2010 to join Creighton University as the men's head basketball coach. Jerry is a season ticket holder and an avid fan of college basketball. He even offered his farm to the Creighton basketball program as a place to come and relax. Coaches, staff, and players were welcomed to go fishing, ride four-wheelers, and escape the daily grind and pressure of Division I athletics.

Over the years of getting to know Jerry, I've learned we have a few things in common. We were both raised in small Iowa towns. Growing up in these Mayberry R.F.D.-like towns influenced our values in similar ways. We were also raised by hardworking, middle-class parents who put family first. In addition, we've had our share of low points and high points throughout our lives.

Jerry's analogy of surviving and thriving on the roller coaster of life is spot on. As a men's basketball coach, I've had to learn how to deal with losing, bad calls, disappointment, and even booing from the home crowd. I've also enjoyed the thrills of winning, seeing my players succeed, and hearing thundering applause and cheers from the crowd.

Jerry's book aligns with my philosophy of coaching young men. It's only when you face adversity that you find out what you're made of.

When you're competing at a high level, you must look back and examine losses and setbacks to figure out what went wrong. At the same time, you need to have a short memory and move onto the next challenge. It's a fine balance. Losing is an opportunity to improve if you look at it the right way.

Another value Jerry writes about, and that I coach, is unselfishness. It's one key to success in life and basketball. I've found that it's much easier to be unselfish when things are going your way and you're winning. Remaining unselfish when you're losing is far more difficult but far more important.

The difference between winning and losing is razor thin. Skills and talent are important, but they don't always guarantee a win. Often what separates the winners from losers is attitude and resilience. Over the years, I've coached young men with elite talent, but who struggle with handling setbacks and contributing as a team player. Basketball and life require teamwork and the ability to survive and learn from the lows.

Jerry's book provides a great game plan to surviving and thriving under any circumstances. He's identified five key points that I agree are vital to surviving downfalls and reaching new highs. You have to allow yourself to have the dream and visualize yourself cutting down the net. Good decisions put you in the right position to capitalize on opportunities. Discipline and determination keep you moving toward your goals when you feel like you have nothing left in the tank. And without question, you must be highly resilient and learn from your setbacks and losses.

Everyone experiences bad calls, losses, and setbacks in the game of life. None of those matter. Only one thing matters. How you respond.

Jerry's book, *Eat Sh*t & Smile: Surviving and Thriving on the Roller Coaster of Life*, is a great illustration of how you respond to life's adversity and what matters most.

—Coach Greg McDermott,
Creighton University, Head Coach, Men's Basketball

A WORD ABOUT THE TITLE

I admit it's a bit crude. I struggled whether to title my first book with such a provocative title. My friends know I'm not a follower of the norm, that I have a habit of saying things bluntly and to the point.

While struggling with potential titles, a favorite saying of mine came to mind: "When you don't know what to say, start with the truth." I've used that truth motto with my kids, grandkids, and those I've mentored for longer than I can recall. Then I started reading some of the old stories I've written over the years when I came across a funny but true story that happened when I was eighteen years old that impacts me to this day. Stay tuned for the details of this story later in my book, but the punch line from that game-changer was "eat shit and smile."

I decided that a significant theme throughout my book would be surviving the potholes of life, so I started using this punch line as my working title. It represented my message, and the story was true, but was the line a good idea?

I shared the working title with family and friends. About 80 percent loved it and 20 percent not so much. Hmmm . . . not what I expected, but it did fit me and aligned with my motto: "When you don't know what to say, start with the truth."

Then I had what I'd call a spiritual experience that I doubt I will ever forget. I had printed out several potential titles on 8½ × 11″ sheets, designing them to look like book covers without photos or graphics but in large black letters. I carried them around for several days and reviewed them at my office, my home, and even at stoplights. Then on Wednesday, November 16, 2022, on Southwest Airlines flight 671 from Dallas to Phoenix, my unforgettable moment occurred. The flight wasn't full, so I chose a seat on the aisle with an empty seat between me and an older lady seated by the window. During the flight, I took the various titles out of my briefcase, studied each of them, then laid them on the seat between us so I could review them again.

I kept trying to determine how the public would view each title and which one would best fit the message I wanted to convey. I remained attracted to *Eat Shit & Smile* but continued to be concerned that it sounded too crass.

When the plane landed, I shuffled all the papers back into my briefcase, standing to retrieve my suitcase from the overhead bin. Noticing the lady near the window starting to gather her purse, I asked her if she needed any help with her overhead luggage. She replied right away, "No. But may I ask you a question?"

"Sure."

"Have you had a rough life?"

I smiled. "Well Ma'am," I replied, "like everyone, I've had my ups and downs, but overall, I've been very blessed. May I ask why you're asking?"

She explained that she had seen my papers, thinking maybe I'd experienced a rough life. I told her I was sorry for what she might have seen and hoped nothing had offended her. "Oh no! Nothing was offensive," she said, "but I think one of your papers was meant for me to see today."

Intrigued, I said, "May I ask you which paper you felt spoke to you?"

I'll be honest. She surprised me when she said, "Eat shit and smile."

"Why do you think that was intended for you?"

She explained she was flying home from Texas after burying her son and needed to hear that message as she went through this trial and wondered about her future. She looked me in the eye and said, "That message was meant for me. I need to accept this difficult season and move forward with my life."

I was blown away. While I processed her comment, the flight attendants hustled us off the plane. I exited quickly, knowing my ride was waiting. I'm disappointed in myself for not getting that woman's name. I should have waited and talked more to her about her story. Ultimately, though, this unexpected spiritual message confirmed that *Eat Shit & Smile* was intended to be my title. If it gave one very sweet mother who had just buried her son one ounce of encouragement, that was enough for me. Done deal!

Crude, offensive, provocative, or just the simple truth of me being me. I give you my book titled *Eat Shit & Smile*.

VIETNAM, PART 1: US EMBASSY SAIGON, 1974

A young Marine wearing polished black shoes and a pressed uniform led me into a large, ornate room with marble floors and fine paintings. The attaché sat at a desk surrounded by flags of each service branch and a large picture of President Nixon.

"Have a seat, Mr. Banks."

I sat down in a small plastic chair positioned in front of his desk. The young Marine moved to the entrance of the door and stood guard opposite another Marine.

The attaché, a small man with a short, businesslike haircut, wore civilian clothes and looked more like an administrator than a military officer.

"Where are you from?" he asked.

"Glenwood, Iowa."

"Never heard of it."

"It's a small town."

"This file shows you're nineteen years old and not in the military—is that correct?"

"Yes, sir."

"From Glenwood, Iowa, to Saigon, Vietnam, in the middle of a war. That's quite the trip. Must be here on some important business."

"Yes, sir. That's correct."

"Have you ever been to Saigon before, Mr. Banks?"

"No, sir."

"Have you ever been out of the United States before?"

"Sir, I've hardly been outside of Iowa before this trip."

He opened a manilla folder, pulled out some documents, and read them in silence. He didn't speak or give any sign of what he was thinking. After what felt like an eternity, he raised his head and looked me in the eye.

"Mr. Banks, I think you're a fucking liar."

My heart started racing. Blood rushed to my face. "Excuse me, sir?"

His voice got louder. "You heard me. I think you're a fucking liar."

No words came out of my mouth. I could only stare at him as my heart rate continued to climb. I wondered if he could see my chest moving under my shirt. How did he know? I wanted to tell him he was right, but I couldn't get any words out.

"You really think I'm gonna buy that you're engaged to some Vietnamese girl you've never met before? Do you think I haven't seen this type of shit before? This is a lie to get her out of the country."

I couldn't believe what was happening. A supposedly quick trip to the embassy to sign some documents had turned into a heated interrogation. He knew exactly what I was up to.

"Unless you tell me the truth right now, there'll be an FBI investigation, and your ass is going to jail. From Glenwood, Iowa, to a prison cell in Saigon. How does that sound, Mr. Banks?"

My mind was racing. FBI investigation? Jail? I was nineteen years old, and my life was about to be ruined. But as much as I wanted to come clean (and I did want to), nothing came out. I just sat there. Frozen.

"Banks, I'm waiting. I don't have time for this shit. It's now or never."

I had tunnel vision. I could only see his angry red face and hear my heart jumping around in my chest. After an excruciating stare-off, he broke eye contact and looked at the two Marines standing guard at the door.

"Get this piece of shit out of my sight."

The next thing I knew, four hands clamped around my body, lifting me out of the chair. My legs felt like lead. The Marines manhandled me toward the door, half dragging me. As they nearly had me through the office door, the attaché yelled for the Marines to stop. They swung me around to face him.

"Banks, while you're in this country, you had better not need us because you're on your own."

He waved his hand toward the door as the marines shoved me out onto a driveway in the heart of Saigon, Vietnam, in 1974, mere months before the city would fall to the Communist regime from the North.

The last words of the embassy attaché yelling I was "on my own" echoed in my mind like a siren. And there I stood, stuck with no support from the US government in a violent, unstable war zone. I wondered if I'd ever see my friends and family again.

INTRODUCTION: CHARTING YOUR HAPPINESS

My name is Jerry Banks, and I'm a storyteller. If I could identify one villain in my narrative, it would be overconfidence in myself. Life has thrown some big curveballs at me, and as much as I've stumbled along the way, I've not only survived; I've thrived. Whenever I've made mistakes, I can see how I was overconfident in my dreams or in myself and didn't do enough research or study. As a young person, I thought I could jump off cliffs and build my wings on the way down. After getting burned several times, I learned balance in my decision-making.

I'm a business guy to my core and have spent my career in real estate investing, crunching numbers and making deals. Over time I've managed over $2 billion in transactions and over three million square feet of property. I've always had an entrepreneurial spirit. At age fourteen, I taught myself how to draw home plans and started getting paid for my work. At age fifteen, I bought, remodeled, and sold a home. I did the same thing with some land at age eighteen, then became the youngest person in Iowa to get a real estate license. I was twenty-four when I started my first company, Century 21 Banks Realty. In my thirties, I owned thirteen pizza franchises.

As great as that all sounds on the surface, my journey has been far from easy. I've dealt with divorce, bankruptcy, and the weight of unresolved family trauma. Now in my sixties, I'm in an amazing place. You might call it peak happiness. But the road to get here was treacherous, and many times I doubted if I would ever reach a place like this. Because I'm a numbers guy who's obsessed with spreadsheets, I started charting my happiness several years ago during a period of deep reflection. Yes, I know a happiness chart seems a bit odd, but we're all a bit odd. I'm just not afraid to share my oddities with the world. Most of them anyway.

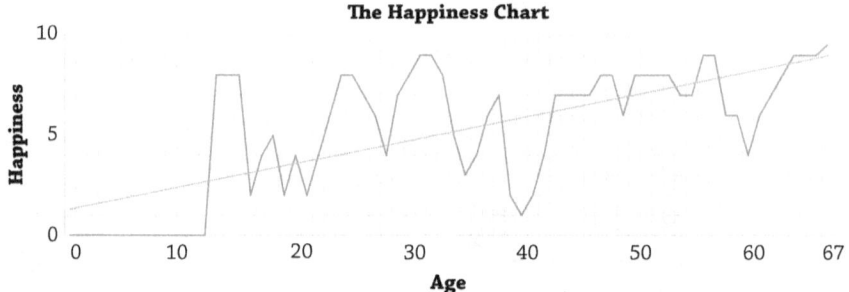

As you can see, my happiness over the years looks like a roller coaster ride with lots of extreme ups and downs. The chart starts at age twelve because that's when most people begin to consider happiness in a more complex way. It's around that age when we become more conscious about happiness.

Today I find happiness in many places—some of them unexpected. Even more than happiness, though, I've found great joy in the process of living, failing, and not chasing happiness, but in exploring the mystery and wonders of living. Throughout this book, when you hear me talking about achieving happiness, in truth, it's more about me (and others) experiencing great joy in this process we call life.

Although I'm known as a business guy, this chart reflects both my business and personal life because, as much as you try, you can't separate the two. One of my greatest joys is helping and seeing other people succeed. From my mentoring to my support of the Women's Fund of

Southwest Iowa and other nonprofits I'm involved in, I want my current chapter in life to be all about giving back.

My goal for everyone I work with is to give back by helping them achieve peace, happiness, and success—a lot more easily than I did. The stories and lessons in this book are for you if you're . . .

- Dreaming of starting your own business.
- Getting started in real estate or some other business.
- Struggling to maintain your momentum as an entrepreneur.
- An employee looking for a greater purpose.
- Feeling lost, like you hit a detour that took you off course.
- Wondering if life's put a "kick me" sign on your back.
- Just looking for a way to achieve greater happiness in life.

You don't have to chart your happiness on a spreadsheet like I did (although if you like spreadsheets, it's kind of fun), but you need to understand where happiness comes from, how to create it, and how to manage it.

Is happiness just a thing that happens to you when life is working in your favor? Is happiness a choice? Can you manipulate your happiness level no matter what unexpected events enter your world? These are all questions we'll explore.

Happiness and success don't require greatness; they come from you understanding the levers you must pull and the tools you must use to create them for yourself. Although I don't believe there is a "system" that fits everyone, I know there are tools and combinations of tools that will work for everyone at any stage of life. The key is knowing which tool to use at the right time. Please allow me to repeat myself because it's incredibly important: Happiness and success don't require greatness.

Both business and life are a roller coaster ride of highs and lows, so it's important to get the most out of the ride called your life. Although you cannot control every twist and turn in your journey, you can set yourself up for the best ride possible.

WHY WRITE SOMETHING SO PERSONAL?

Some will wonder, or perhaps even be critical of, why I published a book that exposes all my personal, and sometimes ugly, stories from the past. It's a valid question, so let me explain. First off, I've noticed that to a degree, many people live in false perceptions these days because of social media and the press. As a society, we're exposed, or perhaps bombarded, by the press and social sites such as Facebook, X (formerly known as Twitter), Instagram, LinkedIn, and more with self-authored vignettes of the lives of our acquaintances and people we follow.

Right or wrong, much of the time they promote images of how perfect and wonderful their lives, kids, husbands, or wives are. Rarely does anyone post about the imperfect sides of their life. The net effect is that we often come away feeling we're among the few, rare, or only ones who have all this garbage in our life. We feel like we're the only ones with a bull's-eye painted on our backside.

I've grown tired and exasperated by this false pretense and feel like it does real damage. I know that, in reality, everyone has skeletons in their closet they wish remained hidden. If I can serve as an example of reality, maybe I can help someone else see that what they're going through isn't unique or unusual. I want people to learn and realize that when they feel as though they're on the downward slope or at the bottom of the roller coaster, they're not alone. I've been there, and so has everyone else.

I hope that by exposing my roller coaster of a lot of life-shattering downs and a lot of amazing ups, I can serve as an example that there is life after the fall. You just have to learn how to survive, be resilient, and eat shit and smile.

MR. COLWELL'S ADVICE

In 1973 the Iowa legislature changed the requirements to get a real estate license from age twenty-one to age eighteen. The law would take effect on the first of July. I turned eighteen in February and found that I could take the test in March, but if I passed, I couldn't get the license until July 1. In March, I made the 145-mile drive to Des Moines and took the Iowa Real Estate Salesman Exam. That was my only option. Back in those days, we had no internet. "Online" was something you did with wet clothes to get them to dry.

A few weeks later, I received a notice by snail mail that I'd passed. When I called the real estate commission, they informed me I could pick up my license at their offices, or they would mail it to me sometime thereafter. On July 1, I was at their office door first thing in the morning as they unlocked it. I had to wait while they typed my license. After handing it to me, the friendly clerk told me I was the youngest person in Iowa to hold a real estate license. Not a bad start to adulthood, I thought.

A few weeks after receiving the license, I stopped by the local Southside Café to grab lunch. The place was packed, so I took the only empty seat at the counter, settling in without noticing who was sitting next to me. It wasn't until I placed my order that I recognized the man to my right: Bert Colwell, our small-town real estate icon.

Mr. Colwell was in his late sixties and reflected the stereotypical real estate and insurance agent of that era. He wore a black suit with a starched white long sleeve shirt and a thin black tie. His heavy gold watch, matching gold ring, gold cuff links, and a gold tie clip displayed further signs of his success. The man loved his gold.

I didn't dare speak to him. This man was where I wanted to be someday. What could I say to him that would be of interest? I sat quietly, avoided eye contact, and waited for my ham on rye. It wasn't until after the waitress served my iced tea and I thanked her that he turned his head and looked at me. My cover was blown. I could feel his stare, but I didn't dare turn my own head.

"You're the Banks kid, aren't you?"

Shit, he recognized me. I turned and faced him.

"Yes, Mr. Colwell, I'm Jerry Banks, and Lloyd is my father."

An awkward silence followed. Turning his head back to his meal, he continued to eat as if nothing had happened. I was a nervous wreck. Should I try to make further conversation? He'd spoken to me. He knows who I am. Should I just keep quiet? Maybe I should excuse myself to the bathroom and never come back.

Without looking at me, Mr. Colwell broke the silence with his aged and gravelly voice.

"Your old man tells me you just got your real estate license. Some kind of record or something."

I'm sure my voice betrayed my nervousness.

"Yes, I did sir."

He mumbled a "harrumph" and started eating again.

I prayed he wouldn't ask me anything else. Several minutes later, he spun around on his stool, his entire body facing me.

"Kid, do you want to know what the secret to success is in real estate?"

"Sure, Mr. Colwell. I'd love to know the secret."

He took a toothpick out of his mouth with one hand and with the other threw a couple of bucks and some loose change on the counter. Looking me in the eye for the first time, he said, "Kid, your success in real estate depends on how much shit you can eat every day and keep on smiling."

Wow. I didn't expect him to say anything like that! Something about hard work, grinding it out, doing your research would have made sense. But eating shit? And smiling? I searched my mind for an intelligent response. Before I could get anything out, he stood up, slapped my shoulder, and walked out of the café.

That was it? The secret to real estate success? Eat shit and smile? I sat and stared at my sandwich, wondering what he meant. After several minutes, the lesson dawned on me. You take a lot of shit in the real estate business, and how you respond is the key to success. Maybe there was something to what he said.

Later that night, I told my dad about my encounter with Mr. Colwell. He got a good laugh out of it. But for me, it became more than a funny observation from a grizzled real estate veteran. I thought about his advice for days, weeks, and months, and I still think about it today—decades later.

A few days after getting Mr. Colwell's advice, I was navigating a difficult real estate transaction when his words entered my mind. Remembering Mr. Colwell's stark wisdom had me go from feeling the burden of the moment to feeling more positive, enabling me to press on into my new career. "Jerry," I said to myself, "you just gotta make this work. Eat shit and smile." I closed the deal instead of giving up in frustration. This philosophy was a nugget of gold from a wise man, and I knew that metaphorically eating shit and smiling could serve me for a long time.

Little did I know, however, that Mr. Colwell's advice would be useful not just in my business but in my personal life as well. Over the next fifty years, I learned how to exercise the lesson more times than I wished. Through the peaks and valleys of my roller coaster life, I've often had to eat shit and smile.

If you're actively taking part in the human world, you've likely been served your fair share of shitty situations. Everyone lives a roller coaster life of ups and downs—some minor, some life-changing. Although the philosophy of eating shit and smiling made sense to me initially, understanding is one thing; living it is another.

Mr. Colwell taught me a valuable lesson that day, but he didn't teach me how to live it. He gave me a mental reframe, which has been valuable. An "eat shit and smile" philosophy is all about what you do when difficult things happen in life, enabling you to stay positive and keep moving forward with what matters most. The "keep moving forward" part is most important because staying positive is easier said than done.

In this book, I'm adding to Mr. Colwell's advice by giving you some tools to live by his tough-love philosophy. These tools will also give you inputs for what I call your own internal GPS system that will help show you the way through the ups and downs of your personal and professional life. In upcoming chapters, I'll teach you . . .

- How to get into a positive mindset when things go bad.
- How to get back on track when life throws you off your path.
- What to do when your back is full of arrows, and you don't feel you can take another step forward.

Ultimately, of course, I'll teach you how to eat shit, keep smiling, and grow. That's what this book is all about.

CHAPTER 1

YOUR INTERNAL GPS SYSTEM

*"Go confidently in the direction of your dreams.
Live the life you've imagined!"*

—Henry David Thoreau

In 1983 Korean Air flight 007 was en route from Anchorage, Alaska, to Seoul, South Korea. The pilots made an error in their navigation calculations that caused the plane to enter Soviet Union airspace. The Soviets thought it was an intruding United States spy plane and sent fighter jets to intercept it. The Soviet jets fired warning missiles toward the plane. Flight 007's pilots either missed or misunderstood the situation and continued their course.

The Soviets responded by shooting down the plane, killing all 269 passengers and crew, including Congressman Larry McDonald of Georgia. This set off one of the most intense moments in the Cold War between the United States and the Soviet Union. Both sides viewed the incident as an act of provocation and perhaps an act of war.

For several years, the relationship between the United States and the Soviet Union remained tense until an investigation revealed the truth about what happened. The pilots made a navigation error and went off course. The Soviet Union made an error in their decision to shoot down the plane based on the fear the aircraft was a US spy plane.

Both were tragic human errors.

As a result, President Ronald Reagan ordered a speedup in the development and implementation of the military's Global Positioning Systems (GPS). In 1988 GPS was operational worldwide and made available to the public at no cost. Today our dependence on GPS navigation is a routine part of our lives. GPS not only tells us where we are, but it shows us how to get to our desired destination using the most efficient path. You simply input your destination, and GPS leads you turn by turn.

What does this have to do with you?

I believe everyone has a very refined GPS system in their DNA. I call it your internal GPS system. Your internal GPS system is more sophisticated than the one on your smartphone, yet there are no satellites to coordinate your life destination and map out the precise path. Despite the lack of satellite support, your internal GPS will take you to your desired destination—but only when you give it the correct inputs.

The problem is you can't physically see your internal GPS system, and you don't have a keyboard to input your destinations. Your GPS system is far more elusive, sophisticated, and sensitive than a device. But isn't that true about us as humans? Aren't we far more complex, elusive, and sophisticated than any piece of hardware?

My goal is to show you how your internal GPS system is not as difficult to use as you may think. All you have to know are a few programming tricks. Ultimately, your internal GPS can lead you to your destiny with the proper inputs, but first you need to understand how to access and use it. That starts with refining the inputs you give it.

This refining process can be challenging, but it's always worthwhile. You're not using your internal GPS to travel to a location fifteen minutes or several hours away. You need it to reach your desired destination in ten, twenty, thirty, or even forty years. Keep in mind, the destination it takes you to isn't always physical in nature. Typically, a combination of both the physical and internal worlds will define your life.

The first step to accessing your internal GPS is learning to believe in it. We do this with our body every waking hour. We accept and use our eyes, our ears, our arms, and our legs. Can you imagine not accepting and believing in your left leg? Dragging that leg behind you would be exhausting. Or imagine not accepting and using your arms. Picking up objects with your teeth wouldn't be very efficient. We see the parts of our body, and we accept them, so we naturally exercise and use them daily. You must adopt the same belief in your internal GPS system to get the most out of it.

It's true; you can't see it, so your internal GPS is more difficult to accept. But I believe we all have an internal GPS system that's wired into each of us and lives within our DNA. We know the brain sends signals throughout the body. Once you understand that the brain transmits signals, it's easier to imagine you can influence, to some extent, which signals the brain sends to your internal GPS. Researchers in the field of hypnosis study the power of suggestion. While my book isn't about hypnosis, it's my theory that similar elements are involved because when you enter particular inputs into your internal GPS system, you're triggering similar mechanisms triggered in hypnosis.

I'm where I am in life today because I turned on my GPS at age nineteen. A series of disasters shook me into realizing that I needed to change or remain miserable. I wasn't sure what I was doing when I started programming my GPS system, and I didn't consider it a GPS system then (that concept didn't exist yet), but I was using it like one. At age twenty-four, I started feeding my internal GPS regularly. By age forty-two, I started to believe it was real and recognized how it could serve me. Now, in this season of my life, I've seen the results, have refined the inputs, and can't wait to share them with you.

Through decades of experimenting and testing my own internal GPS system, I've identified five foundational inputs you need to know to help you get the most out of your internal GPS system and maximize your results, as well as your happiness in life. I call these inputs **The 4 Ds + 1: Dreaming, Decisions, Determination, Discipline + Resilience**.

Ready to tap into the power of your internal GPS system and achieve your best life? I'll break down these five inputs and show you how to use each to program your internal GPS to guide you in business and in life. I promise you it's a fun, rewarding journey, and with the right follow-through, it will change your life and business in ways you never imagined possible.

Buckle up. Here we go!

DREAMING: THE FIRST D

Your internal GPS must know where you want to go before it can start working, and the most important input for that is dreaming. The only rule is you must believe in the dreams you dream. This means you must visualize yourself achieving and living that dream.

Electricity is the energy source for the GPS in your car or smartphone, and interestingly enough, it's the same for your Internal GPS. Our cells conduct electrical currents. Your nervous system requires electrical impulses to send signals throughout your body and to your brain, making it possible for you to move, think, and feel. When you dream, you're sending electrical messages to your brain just like inputting data sends messaging to your GPS.

A great example of this comes from successful athletes. They visualize performing with excellence in multiple situations. Programming high performance into their internal GPS gives them confidence that their goal is possible. The process often manifests itself into elite performances. Although that's a short-term example of dreaming, the same mechanism is at play for both short- and long-term dreams.

Did you ever wake up from a dream and marvel that everything that happened in your dream felt very real? That's because it was, at least as far as your mind is concerned. Your brain does not decipher where it gets its information from. Mostly, information comes from your five senses: your smell, sight, touch, sound, and taste. But your senses just gather information for your brain. You don't really see with your eyes. You see with your brain. If you close your eyes and picture a palm tree, for example, you can actually see a palm tree. You didn't need your eyes to get a clear picture of a palm tree in your mind.

Over the years, I've learned from my daughter Kelley that gymnasts are masters at visualization. Kelley herself was an award-winning gymnast from a very young age through college. She's now the Elite Program Director for the Omaha Gymnastics Academy. Kelley tells me that when a gymnast learns a backflip, she will drill each part of the skill: the takeoff, the flip, and the landing. An athlete repeats drills like this over and over to learn the correct technique to accomplish what she wants. Then she works the skill over and over—with a spot, into a pit, and eventually on her own. Repetition creates a neural pathway in her brain, and each repetition deepens or strengthens that neural pathway. Eventually a gymnast no longer has to think of the takeoff, rotation, and landing. Instead, she just thinks "backflip," and her brain takes her along all the steps without having to think about each step individually.

Another value of visualization: Doing skills over and over creates wear and tear on your body, so athletes practice visualization to help protect their bodies. Instead of doing fifty backflips every day, a gymnast can picture themselves doing five backflips in between each repetition. That means the athlete physically completes ten backflips per day, but her neural pathways for that skill are altered by five times that amount! As the gymnast practices the skill and practices visualization, her brain starts to interpret the images in her brain and fires the proper muscles in her body as if she's actually doing the skill.

Understanding that you can mentally practice steps that will make you successful with any endeavor can change your life incredibly. You can visualize speeches you want to give, conversations you'd like to have, or simply visualize the life you want to live and the steps you're going to take to make it happen. One thing most successful people have in common is their belief that they will be successful long before they actually achieve a particular success. They just know, deep down, that they will fulfill their dream.

When you can visualize your dream and the steps to get there, over and over, you will create the neural pathways in your brain to be successful. Heading down that path will eventually become an expected outcome, rather than a far-off dream. It will help you overcome setbacks and achieve your goals.

The more consistent you are with your dreams, the more your nervous system delivers the correct message to the brain. Consistently telling yourself where you want to go, who you want to be, and what you want your life to be about is crucial. Activating and loading your internal GPS with specific dreams as much as you can reinforces your system to focus on opportunities that will get you there, and often faster. You can always change and move toward a new dream—that's okay. But when you're pursuing a specific dream, you need to focus on directing yourself in its direction.

Does this sound like some newfangled idea? Maybe, but I assure you it's not. It's simply a new way of framing an age-old truth. Leaders, as far back as the Roman Empire, championed the concept of "you are what you think and dream."

Emperor Marcus Aurelius wrote in his series of books *Meditations*, "The happiness of your life depends upon the quality of your thoughts." He also wrote, "Very little is needed to make a happy life. It is all within yourself, your way of thinking. Our life is what our thoughts make it."[1]

Fast forward more than two centuries to the genius inventor of all things Apple: Steve Jobs. In his 2005 Stanford commencement address he said, "You can't connect the dots looking forward; you can only connect them looking backward. So you have to trust that the dots will

---

[1] Marcus Aurelius, *Meditations*, trans. Gregory Hays (Modern Library, 2002), 17.

somehow connect in your future. You must trust in something—your gut, destiny, life, karma, dreams, whatever. This approach has never let me down, and it has made all the difference in my life."[2]

I can look back at my life and see evidence that I dreamed about someday representing a famous or wealthy individual in their real estate investments in the early 1980s when I first started taking classes related to investment real estate known as the CCIM courses. I consistently dreamed and visualized my role in this potential endeavor over and over. Little did I realize that in 1992 this consistent dream would become reality. Something similar can happen for you if you follow the process I'm about to share with you.

DECISIONS: THE SECOND D

Every day you're confronted with choices. Do I get out of bed now or sleep for another hour? Should I attend another seminar? What book should I read next? What should I eat for lunch? Who should I hang out with this weekend? Can I afford this house, this car, or this vacation?

It's important to understand and respect the impact of your decisions. For your internal GPS system to serve you to its maximum potential, the decisions you make are crucial. Even what may seem like minor decisions can completely change your course. I'm comfortable admitting I've made a lot of poor decisions, which I'll share more about throughout my book. The most important thing to keep in mind is that making good decisions will take you toward your dreams, while bad ones could take you in the opposite direction. You may think this seems obvious, but putting the right decision-making process into practice and knowing when to redirect is a different animal when you're in the

---

[2] Steve Jobs, "'You've got to find what you love,' Jobs says." *Stanford Report*, Stanford University, June 12, 2005, https://news.stanford.edu/stories/2005/06/youve-got-find-love-jobs-says.

actual game of life. Here's a critical point: Your internal GPS knows when you're making decisions that are counter to your dreams.

For example, if your dream is to become a pilot, you have a dream. Now you must make good decisions to make that a reality. That will involve taking courses, signing up for pilot school, and more. If you're not doing the things that get you closer to your dream, your internal GPS knows you don't really want it that much. It only operates on the inputs you give it. If your inputs are to sign up for class and study two hours every day, it will keep you on course. If your inputs are to skip studying to hang out with friends, play video games, or get lost in social media, your system will react to those inputs, and your dream of becoming a pilot will always remain just a dream.

My favorite example of how decisions connect with dreams and your internal GPS relates to picking your team in life. The people you choose to surround yourself with make a massive impact on your ability to achieve your dreams. Hall of Fame NFL linebacker Ray Lewis's biggest message to young people is the importance of your teammates. "You show me your crowd," he says, "and I will show you your future!" Lewis says you need three types of people in your crowd: "the inspired, the excited, and the grateful." Then he says you should grade every person in your crowd by those values. If they don't fit, then you cut them out of your crowd.[3]

With whom you decide to associate is a vital decision. Are the people in your circle adding value to you in a way that gets you closer to achieving your dreams? Who is draining your time and energy and not adding value? Do you have people distracting you, pulling you off course, and blocking you from being the person you want to be? What faces and names are popping into your mind right now that you know aren't helping you achieve your dreams? You know who they are.

---

[3] "One of the Greatest Speeches Ever | Ray Lewis," YouTube video, uploaded by Motivation-Hub, January 30, 2018, https://www.youtube.com/watch?v=W8hVRUCizGk.

They might be a blast on Friday night, but they only care about the next party and aren't helping you advance.

What should you do? Maybe you've known these people or this person for years or decades. You can't just cut them out of your life forever. You can, but that's difficult for most people. If you don't want to cut them out of your life, you must, at a minimum, set boundaries on their influence. If they're negative, dismiss your dreams, and tell you your ideas are stupid, ask yourself why. Many times, these types of people have given up on their dreams and don't want others to seek theirs. It's true: Misery loves company.

Choosing the right team and cutting bad teammates is often the hardest thing to do on your journey to achieving your dreams. We're a social species, and we're loyal. This book contains many lessons about decisions, but this is one of the most important, so I want to offer more than a "you should do this." I'll tell you what I share with people whom I consider my friends.

I say, "I'm going to tell you something. A true friend tells you what you need to hear, not what you want to hear. And I want to be your true friend, so I'll share what I think is working for you and what I think you need to fix. Not to criticize or act superior, but because I want to be your friend. When I'm finished, I'd like you to do the same for me."

Giving them the opportunity to express their perspective is important. Open and honest conversations are two-way. How the other person responds to your proposition will tell you a lot about what kind of person they are. If they're willing to see where the conversation goes, then perhaps they can remain on your team, and maybe even become one of your greatest teammates in life. If they attack you, dismiss you, or refuse to talk, then you probably know everything you need to know about them. My personal policy is I will unfollow, unfriend, or un-family anyone who consistently drains my soul. I wasn't always that way, but it's where I'm at now, and although it may seem harsh, the policy was developed and tested for decades before I finally adopted it. I only wish I'd done it sooner in life.

Your internal GPS is always working, but you must work with it, not against it. When you surround yourself with people who are counter to your dreams, you're setting your GPS off course by giving it bad inputs. On the one hand, you're directing your internal GPS toward who you want to be and where you want to go. On the other hand, you're receiving input from people who promote the opposite of your dream and suggest a different course. Often they're distracting you or taking you off course deliberately. Your internal GPS knows when you're serious about a dream. Make sure your decisions are feeding it inputs that support and move you closer to your dreams.

DETERMINATION: THE THIRD D

Determination is the ability to continue to try doing something despite the difficulty. It's a form of not giving up and seeing things through. Think of determination as mile markers on your highway of progress.

First you have a dream. Then you decide to pursue that dream. Determination is the refusal to stop doing what you need to do to arrive at your destination. When detours and roadblocks interrupt your path, it's your ability to stay determined and keep pushing forward that gets you to the finish line.

I remember a colleague saying that 80 percent of success is showing up. I think there's an element of truth to that, but I question the 80 percent number. I would put it more like 50 percent. I've noticed that many people show up consistently but don't achieve much. Yes, you must show up, but it's equally important to have the determination to do what's necessary and keep moving forward when you show up and things don't go your way. To win the game, you have to keep playing hard, even when you're losing. You can't just show up and hope it works out in your favor.

Determination has always meant moving forward, even as I acknowledged the product called "me" will never be perfect.

Personal development is not a destination; it's an ongoing process that never ends. You must be determined to grow, and to grow, you have to continually work on areas of weakness.

One of the best examples of determination I always emphasize to entrepreneurs I mentor is having the determination to treat others well. Caring about people is low-hanging fruit that doesn't take any specialized training. Tending to your relationships always pays off big in both business and life, yet paying close attention to how you treat your customers, your family members, and your friends is often left hanging on the tree of opportunity, especially if you're too focused on your own success.

Treating others with respect and dignity is synonymous with having good manners. People associate good manners with knowing which fork to use at the dinner table or remembering to put the napkin on their lap. Those things fall more under etiquette than manners. Etiquette is a code of conduct and societal rules that govern social behavior. These rules are more formal and specific. Manners are behaviors that reflect your attitude.

Columnist and author Emily Post said this about the dual nature of manners in her book *Etiquette*: "Good manners reflect something from the inside—an innate sense of consideration for others and respect for self."[4]

Manners not only reflect your attitude but also affect the attitudes of those you interact with. Using good manners in a work environment is akin to regularly putting motor oil in your car's engine. It lubricates the work environment and makes everything run a lot smoother. I've found that even saying simple things like "thank you," "please," and "you're welcome," not only adjusts my own mood but makes whomever I interact with more open to my ideas and viewpoints. Treating people well leads to more productive and meaningful conversations because being polite and respectful removes defense barriers.

---

[4] Emily Post, *Etiquette: In Society, in Business, in Politics and at Home* (Cosimo, Inc., 2007), 579.

When I managed teams, I consistently discussed the importance of good manners in staff meetings. I'd propose "good manners" challenges. Use good manners for a full week and report back to me. Everyone who remained determined to see the challenge through always reported excellent results.

Good manners should go beyond the office too. They should be standard behavior when addressing people at drive-up windows, stores, and any place you find yourself interacting with another person. I have an embarrassing confession. I used to be terrible at showing good manners when I ordered at drive-up windows. My attitude cried out, "Just give me my food. I'll give you the money, and we can all be on our way." I didn't want or feel the need for small talk.

My daughters changed my view and attitude toward that behavior. More than a few times, I would leave a drive-up window and receive comments from my girls about my rudeness. My response was always something like, "I wasn't rude. I didn't say a word." I'd go right into defensive mode.

They'd correctly point out that not saying anything was, in fact, rude and dismissive of the person serving me. A simple thank you and smile was all I needed to say or do. In my daughters' eyes, by not practicing good manners, I was being rude and arrogant—and they were right! Eventually I listened because I know they love me and care about how others perceive me. Over time I adapted my behavior to treat those workers with kind words. You never know whom you might encounter in those moments or what burdens they may carry. Kindness is helpful, and using good manners with everyone, regardless of their position, is the right thing to do.

Most of business and life revolve around relationships and interactions with others. Many of your dreams depend on getting along with people and receiving their help. One thing you can start doing today to increase your chances of achieving your dreams is be determined to have good manners with every individual you encounter in life, inside and outside of your work environment.

DISCIPLINE: THE FOURTH D

Discipline is the mental ability to follow through with actions that support your dreams and goals. Don't get this confused with determination, which is staying committed to getting through detours and difficulties. With discipline, often no real detours or roadblocks impede your progress. You may create mental roadblocks and allow yourself to become distracted, but those are internal creations.

Let's bring this back to your internal GPS system. The distance between dreams and reality is often related to discipline, which I view as the ability to control a mental activity. Controlling a mental activity requires the insight to tie discipline back to your internal GPS. Tying discipline back to your GPS is an important step because your subconscious knows you better than you know yourself. When you set a destination in your GPS, then go off course, it will eventually determine if you're committed to that dream. Staying disciplined shows your GPS that you are serious about your dream.

RESILIENCY: THE PLUS ONE

Dictionary.com shows three definitions for resilience:

1. The power or ability of a material to return to its original form, position, etc., after being bent, compressed, or stretched; elasticity.
2. The ability of a person to adjust to or recover readily from illness, adversity, major life changes, etc.; buoyancy.
3. The ability of a system or organization to respond to or recover readily from a crisis, disruptive process, etc.

Since I am very unlikely at my age to return to my original form, I will go with definition number two. And why do we need this "R" word to reach our dreams? Because your ability to recover from adversity is the most important factor in achieving your dreams. You can have a wonderful dream. You can make good decisions. Your determination and discipline can work together to move you consistently toward your dream. Everything can be on course with the destination in sight when suddenly a detour sends you flying off course, despite your best efforts to correct your steering.

You may wake up, for example, and find yourself lying at the bottom of a canyon, sunk to the bottom of the abyss with everything you worked toward seemingly out of reach. When this happens, and it happens to the best of us, only your resiliency will get you out of the canyon and back on course. Being resilient in the toughest of times is practicing the philosophy of eating shit and smiling.

I've had several events in my life where I needed resiliency to get me through to the next day. I share many of them with you in this book. I'll start with the first one that took place when I was sixteen. For decades, I tried to ignore the impact it had on me. It was only through resiliency that I could eventually reflect and heal.

I'd gone home early in the day to change my clothes after spilling gasoline on my pants at our family business maintenance facility. When I entered my basement room, I heard a noise in the adjacent storage room. Although I was in a hurry, the situation seemed strange, so I entered the storage room to investigate.

To my horror, I found my mom standing on a chair with a noose around her neck. Rushing toward her, I climbed on a chair and removed the noose as she tried her best to fight off my efforts. I remember yelling at her, "Why are you doing this?"

My mom was bawling and shaking as I led her into our basement family room. I sat her down and tried to collect myself. Mom was crying, but without words or explanation, and I, a sixteen-year-old, had no idea what to say. I didn't know what to do either, so I led her to my car and drove her to my father's office. When we arrived, Mom walked straight into a back office. I found Dad and told him we needed to step outside. Then I told him what happened. He thanked me and told me to go back to work.

My parents never mentioned that day's events again. Not a word. I was angry for a long time. I thought no sixteen-year-old should have to witness that. I wanted to ask Mom, "Why the hell did you do that to me?" But I never asked. Instead, I did a great job of sweeping it under the rug, just as my parents' silence about the matter was telling me what to do.

That moment affected my relationship with my mother for the next fifty years. We remained close. I always treated her with kindness and respect, but I couldn't erase what I saw that day, nor understand how she could attempt such a thing.

It wasn't until I discussed that day with a therapist at age sixty-four and finally opened up about that moment that my perspective changed. Looking back through my adult eyes decades later, I could see the hard journey my mom had traveled and how much she suffered, which potentially played a large part in leading her to attempt suicide when I was just a teenager.

Mom grew up incredibly poor. Her father died when she was three. Her mother died when she was fifteen. She moved to a rooming house and had to work at a restaurant for morning and evening meals. Her older brothers and her sister had abandoned her. She had no one there to help her. I can't image how shattered her world was and the life-altering, unresolved trauma she carried from those days.

With such a tragic childhood, it's no surprise my mother suffered from depression. I saw that in hindsight. I began to understand the depths of her sad beginning, and that allowed me to quit internalizing my own pain and making it all about me. As I processed all my emotions, I found my first big lesson in forgiveness, learning that forgiveness is a gift you give yourself and not necessarily somebody else. That lesson took me fifty years, and only through emotional resilience was I able to push through a painful misunderstanding and judgment toward my own mother and learn to forgive her for attempting suicide.

In hindsight, I think I had a chip on my shoulder toward my mom. While I loved her, I had an underlying anger for her hardness that I never had toward my father. She was always the disciplinarian, hitting first and asking questions later. More than once I got a willow stick or yardstick to the butt for something I'd done or not done. Of course, I only recall the ones I didn't deserve. As a parent, I've now learned those are the ones kids remember the most!

One day she'd driven to the grocery store. After leaving the store, I jumped in the back seat. Since this was well before seat belts or child seats, as Mom drove around the first corner, the back door flew open, and I fell out onto the street. The next thing I knew, Mom was holding me up in the air by one arm and spanking me, all the time yelling, "Don't play with the door handle!"

I have no idea if I had been playing with the handle or not, but I do recall she didn't show one ounce of sympathy or ask me if I was okay. As an adult looking back, I now consider her reaction as one that likely came out of fear that I'd been hurt. Once she realized I was okay, her fear exploded into a good old whipping. I laugh about this event on occasion as I know that today if that happened to a four-year-old boy, the mom could be headed to jail.

I also knew that if I wanted a hug, I needed to wait until Dad got home. My mom was not the hugging type. In my early youth, Dad worked on the railroad and was sometimes gone on the road for two to three days at a time. I recall aching for him to get home so I could hug him, and he could hug me. Mom's attempted suicide was a decisive event for me to put a cap on my feelings toward my mother, protect myself from more hurt, and to stop trying. Instead, I chose to shut down, for the most part, from showing love or expecting love in return from my mom. Respect and care for her, sure. Show love or expect love? Nope.

My mother died January 16, 2024. I'm so grateful she lived long enough for me to see things differently. For the last five years of her life, I talked to her daily and saw her weekly. Every phone call or visit ended with words we hadn't said to each other for decades: "I love you."

In this chapter, I've introduced the concept of your internal GPS system and the tools you'll use to get the most out of it. As you continue to read, you'll discover the power of how those tools and specific inputs can help you take the "eat shit and smile" philosophy and make it work for you in business and life.

CHAPTER 2

LEARN TO DREAM

"You have to dream before your dreams can come true."

—A.P.J. Abdul Kalam

VIETNAM: PART 2

During the summer of 1974, I was nineteen years old and just over a year out of Glenwood High School. The draft just ended, Richard Nixon had resigned from the outfall of Watergate, and President Ford was the new president. I was single, making good money selling real estate, drinking, and partying to excess.

Larry, my older brother by seven years, had recently married a woman named Yolanda (Yoly), who was born and raised in Saigon. He met and married her while stationed in San Francisco as a Marine. After Larry finished his service, they moved back to Glenwood.

One day Yoly presented me with an idea—something that would change the course of my life. She wanted my help to get her younger sisters out of Saigon. I'd go to Vietnam to sign papers that said I was engaged to marry her middle sister Corrina. After that, we'd also be able to get her youngest sister Suzy out of the country. What was in it for me? An all-expense paid trip to Southeast Asia. Being a cocky nineteen-year-old, all I could see it for was a free vacation and adventure. Get the hell out of Glenwood for a bit. What could go wrong? I said yes.

I assumed I'd go in, hang out for a week, sign some papers, and be on my merry way. My parents didn't see it the same way when they learned about this "adventure." But the more they resisted, the more I was determined to go.

On Sunday morning, November 3, 1974, Larry and Yoly drove me from Glenwood to the Omaha, Nebraska, airport. On the way, my brother told me that if anything bad happened, I should call or get to the US embassy because they were there to help US citizens. Yoly told me to talk to her oldest sister Carol if I had any problems.

On the way to Saigon, I needed to stop in San Francisco to visit the Vietnamese consulate's office and get my seven-day visa. Mr. Stinard, an older man who helped me at the office, was very tall and thin, wore greased-back hair and a thin little mustache. I still remember his black suit, white shirt, and thin black tie that complimented his mustache.

"Why the hell are you going to Vietnam?" he asked me.

"I'm going there to get engaged to a young lady," I replied, flashing a confident smile. He didn't look impressed.

"Son, I'm going to give you some advice. No matter what, you make sure you get out of that country before this visa expires. If you stay longer than seven days, your government cannot help you. Understand?"

"Yes sir, understood."

Dramatic, I thought, but he probably had to say that to everyone.

My flight landed in Saigon on schedule, and Yoly's sisters Carol, Corrina, and Suzy greeted me at the arrival gate. All three were very cheerful, warm, and welcoming. My mini vacation to Southeast Asia was off to a good start, so I thought.

The drive from the airport to their home took about an hour and gave me my first glimpse of what I'd soon see on a more imposing scale—a country, city, and people ravaged by war. Overturned cars, damaged buildings, severely injured people begging in the streets. There was nothing tropical or fun about this place. I'd seen none of this suffering in the travel brochure I'd created in my head and soon realized I was not in Glenwood anymore. I consoled myself by saying, "It's only seven days, Jerry. Only seven days."

The family's house was a two-story concrete block structure on a major boulevard. It was one of the nicer structures in the densely populated shanty town of sorts. Many of the structures were piecemealed together with random boards and rusted scraps of sheet metal. When I stepped out of the car, the air—a mixture of soot and exhaust fumes—immediately overwhelmed me. I could feel it collecting on my face. When I dragged my finger across my cheek and looked, I could see the filth.

The main floor to the house was a garage with a stairwell that led to the second floor. The top of the staircase had a steel cage-like lid on it that was locked with a bar and padlock from the inside. After we entered the second floor, Corrina immediately locked the covering again.

Steel bars protected all the windows on the second floor. The family's father had died years ago, but the mother showed up to greet me. She'd prepared a large feast in my honor. Everything was ready, so we sat down right away at the table with a three-foot-long fish as the centerpiece.

Everyone sat still and looked at me. They were waiting for something. Unsure of the situation, I turned to Corrina seated next to me and gave her a quizzical look.

"You're our guest of honor," she said and pointed to the large fish.

"Thank you," I smiled, still clueless.

"You get to eat the eye," she said and handed me some chopsticks, then flashed a big smile. I looked around the table, and everyone smiled, shaking their heads with encouragement.

I knew how to use chopsticks but had never eaten a fish's eye. There was no way I could refuse, so I dug the chopstick into the head, plucked out the eye, plopped it into my mouth, and swallowed without chewing. I followed that up with a big smile. Everyone applauded as I disguised my disgust.

Later that night, Corrina showed me my small room with no windows and a steel door. Up to this point, I'd said nothing about the prison-like setup in the house, but I couldn't hold it any longer when I realized Corrina would lock me into the room.

"Why are your locking me in?"

"This will help slow down the Viet Cong in case of attack."

In case of attack? From TV news reports back home, I thought the war was winding down. The steel door closed, and I heard the lock click on the other side. I realized the information I'd perceived wasn't so accurate. I was getting an adventure, but not the kind I'd hoped for.

The next day, the plan was for Corrina and I to head to the US embassy. I'd sign the papers or applications their family attorney had obtained for Yoly and her sisters, then lie low for a couple of days and get the hell out of there. I had to sign these documents in person at the embassy offices. I was happy to go there because I recalled my brother telling me the US embassy would take care of me if I needed help. It would be comforting to know where it was located. Plus, when I got back to Glenwood, I'd have a good story to tell my drinking buddies about visiting the US embassy. Or so I thought.

BIG DREAMS CAN START SMALL

The first thing you should know about dreams is they can and often do start small, increasing in size as you grow. But in the beginning, they can be small. It's not the size of the dream that matters when you dream; it's the act of allowing yourself to dream in the first place that's most important.

With that said, I like to dream big and encourage you to do the same. Dreaming big is relative, though, isn't it? If your dead busted broke, homeless, and jobless, the dream of a steady job and roof over your head might be dreaming big. If that's your situation, dream big! When you've already won the lottery of life, however, then dreaming big might look much different. I've heard it said that if your dreams don't scare you, then you're not dreaming big enough. I'd change the wording a bit and suggest that if your dreams don't push you or stretch you, then they aren't big enough. I don't like the word "scare" as I don't want to fear a dream or have fear as the primary driver to accomplish a dream. It feels counterproductive. But I do want your dreams to push and stretch you to do things you never imagined possible.

When you start thinking about dreaming, you might get trapped into thinking you aren't capable of this or that and start dreaming with an undercurrent of negativity. In my experience, most people are way more capable than they give themselves credit for. Give yourself the freedom to explore the pull of your big dreams. Believe in your internal GPS to help guide you to your dreams.

At the time I grew up in Glenwood, Iowa, it had a population of about 4,000 and featured three stoplights, two police cars, thirteen churches, and about fifteen bars. Everyone knew everyone's business, and secrets never remained secrets longer than twenty-four hours. Our community was akin to the 1960s version of Andy Griffith's Mayberry. It was and remains a great place to live and raise a family.

To better understand how my views on life during and after growing up in Glenwood evolved, I think it's useful to show you a glimpse of where my career in real estate all started and how my upbringing influenced my life's direction.

Venturing into real estate was a direct result of my father's entrepreneurial spirit. My dad Lloyd Banks worked as a conductor on the Burlington Railroad. He and my mom Evelyn purchased some land while renting a small apartment in town before I was born. That land became the setting for my childhood.

When Dad purchased the land, it only had one cement block building on it, which looked to be the start of a house that was never finished, then used as an animal shelter. Dad saw that cement block shelter as the genesis of what would become our future home. Working nights and weekends, my parents used their own labor, skills, and ingenuity to turn that animal shelter into a two-bedroom, one-bathroom house. Later they added a garage and workshop.

When I made my debut from the hospital, my new home featured a central oil furnace but no air conditioning. A home with no AC meant finding inventive ways to stay cool. When the summer heat peaked, my refuge was the vinyl floors that laid over the cement slab because they stayed cool. It was a different story in the winter months when they felt like walking on a sheet of ice.

I still smile, recalling huddling around the oil heater trying to warm ourselves in the frigid Iowa winters. My family achieved a significant milestone the year we got a furnace with duct work to every room. Our former home is still there today at 905 Townsend Street in Glenwood.

Outside the house was a large oak tree towering in a field. My dad tied a three-quarter-inch rope around one of the large branches and connected a stuffed burlap bag to the bottom of the rope. For hours on end, we'd swing on that bag. All the neighborhood kids appropriately named it "the bag swing."

We always had a contest to see who could go the highest and fastest around the tree or do tricks. While swinging, we tried things like wrapping our legs around the bag and letting go with our hands, leaning back, or hanging upside down. The trick successfully executed meant you were upright before you slammed into the tree's base. Most of the time, we were successful. But not always.

There were a couple of significant differences between those days and today. Our parents didn't require us to wear safety gear, helmets, or guards. We typically were barefoot, with a pair of shorts or jeans, and maybe a T-shirt. If you didn't land today, you'd be rushed off to the emergency clinic and placed in concussion protocol. In those crazy days, you sucked it up and didn't cry because you knew you would never hear the end. I recall more than once slamming into the bark of the oak tree with a bare back or bare legs and doing my best to suck it up in front of my buddies, especially the older kids.

In the field and barn behind our house lived a beautiful black horse named Midnight. Even when I was the young age of five, my dad allowed me to ride and help care for her. Midnight had three colts that I named Thunder, Lightning, and Julie. One day I found out that Midnight and her colts did not belong to our family. I still recall watching them leave the property in a horse trailer as tears streamed down my face.

Shortly after, the bulldozers showed up. The oak tree was uprooted and removed, along with our bag swing. The barn was demolished. An enormous bonfire consumed many of my young play yard memories. "What the hell?" I thought. My childhood world was destroyed right before my eyes, and nobody asked me how I felt about it. This was my first brush with land development—a rather rough initiation into the real estate world, but I'm over that early trauma now.

What felt like death to my favorite childhood playthings was Dad seeing his dream play out. He'd made a deal to buy the land and worked with the City of Glenwood to extend a street up the hill into the field. My field, barn, horse-riding trail, and bag swing are now Arnold Street in Glenwood. I didn't understand it at the time, but Dad was building a new neighborhood.

He told me just a few years prior to his death at 101 years old that he purchased the land for $20,000 on a contract with $1,000 down and $100 monthly payments. My dad was an entrepreneurial visionary, but he also confessed that he worried he might lose his tail over the deal.

Within a year of buying the property, he found a home builder in Council Bluffs that agreed to help him construct a spec home on a piece of land. He sold that first house to a young couple who became lifelong family friends.

The first Lloyd Banks home sold for $12,000. After that first project in 1961, Dad was able to sell six more homes built on his land. I was six years old when this phase of Dad's career launched, and I was recruited to rake yards and clean out small construction debris. Dad's construction business continued to grow and prosper. Mom became the head bookkeeper, using old school accounting ledgers she kept in place for fifty years. I worked for the family construction business from age six to twenty-four. In the later years of my tenure, I assisted in the family real estate sales business.

I remember Mom and Dad having a motto they'd remind me of periodically: "If you want to eat at the family table, you have to work in the family business." I understood it. If you want to share in the family's blessings, you'd better be helping produce those blessings. Dad worked on both the railroad and in real estate development until I graduated from high school. Mom worked as the family and business bookkeeper, and for several years as a part-time bookkeeper for the town veterinarian.

I didn't realize it growing up, but in hindsight, I can see I came from a blue-collar background that was also entrepreneurial and innovative. The foundation my parents built in me through real-life exposure to both the real estate and construction business was the genesis of my later success. Even more important than the exposure to real estate was witnessing how they treated customers, employees, bankers, vendors, and even competitors. Dad and Mom treated everyone with respect, integrity, and transparency. They showed me it's not just the right way but the only way.

Before I had my driver's license, I learned how to build retaining walls, grade yards with a tractor, and do architectural drafting. By the time I could drive, I spent a summer working with a concrete crew building basements. The next summer I worked with a crew framing homes. I remember shingling a home with wood shake shingles, and I'll never forget carrying the bundles of shingles up a ladder to the second-floor roof. I recall thinking I liked real estate sales a lot better than construction. On top of physical labor, I'd also work a couple of days a week in the office typing contracts, helping with the marketing, advertising, and learning about home sales and finance.

When I was fifteen, my brother Larry and I bought, remodeled, and sold a house in about six weeks. We each made over $2,000 on the project. My senior year in high school I bought a thirty-acre property for $20,000 and flipped it a year later for $30,000.

By my senior year in high school, I was making hourly wages from the family business, doing a few real estate deals, and had some other little entrepreneurial money-making ventures on the side. I could have been making more money than my high school teachers. I had enough money to buy myself a new car at sixteen—a lime green 1969 Opel GT. I knew I'd done something special driving that car around Glenwood. It felt good to see the fruits of my work pay off in a tangible way.

What I realize reflecting on my upbringing was that I was lucky to have parents who not only encouraged dreaming but demonstrated it. My dad showed me how to bring a dream to life. You can't control who your parents are or where you're born, but everyone has the freedom to dream and act on those dreams.

Looking at my dad back when he bought that cement block shelter, nobody would've thought it would be the first step toward developing an entire neighborhood and building a successful real estate business. I'm not even sure if my dad had that vision. But he had a dream of building a home for his family, and once he achieved that dream, it opened his eyes to new possibilities.

THE 9 KEYS TO DREAMING

1. **Dream Big:** Allow yourself to dream and envision what you truly desire. Dreams are the big picture, the ultimate vision of what you want to achieve or experience.
2. **Set Clear Goals:** Break down your dream into achievable goals. Goals are the mile markers on the highway to dream achievement.

3. **Prepare:** As you move toward your goals and dreams, consider what resources may assist you. This could include educational needs, relationships you need to establish, people you need to meet, and subjects you need to research.

4. **Be Resilient:** Not everything will go according to plan. Be prepared to face setbacks, but stay resilient and keep moving forward.

5. **Enjoy the Journey:** Don't forget to enjoy the journey. Appreciate the experiences and lessons learned along the way. Enjoy the process.

6. **Celebrate Achievements:** Celebrate when you reach your goals. This motivates you to continue pursuing your dream. Celebrate those who supported you on your journey. Without them, those achievements may not have occurred.

7. **Stay Flexible:** Adjust your goals or plans as needed. Flexibility can help you navigate unexpected challenges and still reach your dream.

8. **Reflect:** Every year take time to reflect on both your positive experiences and setbacks. Consider what you've learned and how you've grown.

9. **Show Gratitude:** Show gratitude by giving back or paying it forward. Don't just talk about having gratitude. Talk is cheap! Exercise gratitude by giving.

DON'T LET DISTRACTIONS KILL YOUR DREAMS

Dreams without direction are just dreams. If you don't take the next step and add clarity and direction, they'll manifest into anything outside of your head. Distractions kill dreams, and in today's world, you have more distractions than ever before. We live in a world where we're constantly plugged in. Our smartphone has almost become an extension of our bodies. When we hear a chime or feel a vibration, it takes all the willpower we have not to reach for the phone and check.

The smartphone distraction is a battle I fight daily. My daughters, and even my grandkids, lecture me on my distraction. I recognize it's an issue, and I'm working on it. The ironic and sad part about it is when we check, 99 percent of the time what we discover is nothing. We've broken our concentration to see somebody "liked" a post that we liked. You open your email to see five new emails from your favorite brands trying to sell you the next thing. The net effect is negative. If you were working on something important, it takes ten to fifteen minutes to get back into the flow state and accomplish something meaningful.

I receive between 200 and 400 emails a day. No exaggeration. Through my career I've gotten on just about every real estate broker's mailing list in the country. Again, 99 percent of them are email blasts I have no interest in. But my mind (or ego) says there may be one in a million that does interest me, and I need to stay on top of them. What I'm trying to do (emphasis on "trying") is to unsubscribe to those that are in regions of the country where I have no interest. I've also been trying my best to ignore them until the end of the day, then, before leaving my office, going through to delete the ones where the subject line doesn't jump off the page at me.

Keep in mind, I'm not anti-technology. I'm just pointing out today's biggest distraction. Other distractions outside of technology can be just as destructive. They're usually related to lifestyle and have been around since my early days. The biggest distractions that remain are drinking, drugs, and the company you keep.

INSTANT GRATIFICATION THROUGH DISTRACTIONS KILLS DREAMS

As blessed as I was growing up with a template for dreaming, I was not prepared to handle the fruits of success. I always had more money than many of my buddies, which meant I could buy plenty of beer and anything else a teenager would want. It also meant I was set up to fall into the temptation traps for young men with money to blow and no clear vision for the future.

And I did.

To the outside observer, I was a hardworking, good kid. The hidden side of me was living dangerously. I never felt I was an alcoholic, yet every weekend it was not a matter of if I was going to get drunk, it was which beverage and what friends would be involved. Thank God I didn't inherit the gene that makes you an addict, or it could have ruined my life.

The reality was my often-impaired judgment led to dangerous actions like vandalism and thievery. I look back with some embarrassment (and some pride also). Pride because I got by with it, and the events have provided me with some captivating stories to tell over the years. Still, I look back on that chapter of life and wonder what motivated me to such behavior. I think the biggest part of it was the challenge. Could I do it and not get caught?

I ran with a few high school buddies, and together we instigated multiple acts of vandalism and thievery. One significant event involved my high school. We left our mark by spray painting graffiti over significant parts of the school weeks before the annual prom. The principal considered canceling the prom if the perpetrators didn't turn themselves in. We were sure we were going to get caught, so we confessed. Amazingly, there were no serious repercussions. Unfortunately, that only fueled my recklessness even more.

We were also guilty of breaking and entering cars and local businesses. It wasn't because we needed or even wanted the contents. It was simply out of opportunity, challenge, and boredom. I'm sure the beer or whiskey also played a major role. Fortunately, we always evaded capture; otherwise the gravity of some incidents could've warranted felony charges.

At eighteen, I graduated in the lower half of a class of ninety but only because of a couple of breaks along the way. I was a horrible student, unmotivated, and didn't give a damn—mostly because I was making too much money during the day and drinking too much at night.

I wouldn't have graduated had it not been for a compassionate teacher giving me a break I didn't deserve. At the start of my Junior year, I was told I needed one more science credit to graduate. I surmised that the easiest course was Introduction to Chemistry, taught by first-year teacher Mr. Ron Kohn. I only needed a passing grade to graduate. During that semester, I never handed in any assigned homework or passed a single quiz, and I was thrown out of class twice. The teacher was shocked when I recorded a B+ on the final test.

After distributing the test results, he invited me to join him in the back supply room of the chemistry classroom. He told me he knew how I had gotten the B+. He'd reviewed the seating chart and noticed that I sat next to Jon Bliecher, who today is Dr. Jon Bliecher.

"Jerry, I'm going to make you an offer I recommend you accept. I will pass you with a D- so you get your one credit if you make me a promise that you will never take a class from me ever again." We shook hands, and I was able to graduate. Thank you, Mr. Kohn. (May you rest in peace.)

After narrowly escaping high school, applying for college never crossed my mind. I knew my grades would've made me ineligible for most colleges. I'd done the absolute minimum to keep my parents and teachers off my back. Although I knew I was capable of much better, I didn't care.

After high school graduation, I spent the next year and a half in Glenwood continuing my ways: working hard, making good money, and partying way too much. During that time, I also met Karen, who would later become my wife.

I knew I could keep working for the family business and have a good life. Eventually maybe I could even take over as the owner. The downside to that would be people thinking I got everything handed to me. And worse, what if I blew it and the business went under while I was in charge? The more I thought about it, it felt like a lose-lose situation.

I was confident in my abilities. I knew I was good at what I did, but I didn't have a clear dream in my mind about what I wanted my future to look like. As good as things were, I was restless. I thought maybe I just needed to leave Glenwood and do something for myself. But what would that be?

That's when life threw not just one but two hard curveballs at me that finally woke me up. I kept thinking I needed to go somewhere new, try something different. Just get away. The universe listened and delivered the first curveball by sending me to Vietnam.

YOUR GPS INPUT CHECKLIST

- Allowing yourself to dream is the first step.
- Your dreams should pull and stretch you.
- Dreams can start small and grow beyond what you thought was possible.
- Dreams need to be followed by taking action.
- Distractions are dream killers.

CHAPTER 3

MAKE A DECISION

*"Whenever you see a successful business,
someone once made a courageous decision."*

—Peter F. Drucker

VIETNAM: PART 3

I'd just been thrown out of the US embassy and told I was on my own. The US government wouldn't help me. Just the opposite. Now they were looking for a way to throw me in a jail cell.

I looked around the street, trying to find my bearings, when I spotted Corrina walking toward me. After I told her what happened, she drove me back to the house. The entire plan blew up. Now it was a matter of the Viet Cong not attacking and avoiding imprisonment by the US government before I boarded my flight in five days.

That night I lay in my fortified room, remembering the words of the US consulate in San Francisco: "Whatever happens, you better be out of that country in seven days." I had to hang on.

Over the next five days, the family drove me to multiple offices where I signed documents. Every discussion and document were in Vietnamese, and I had no idea what I was signing. I just wanted it to end. I still have vivid color images embedded in my head of terrible things I saw during that week.

On these trips around Saigon, I witnessed up close the ravages of war. I saw children with missing arms and legs who hadn't received any medical treatment. One day near the market, I walked past a man lying on the sidewalk with his back to me. The stench emanating from him was unfamiliar, so after I passed by, I looked back. He was dead and decomposing. Maggots were crawling out of his nose. I gagged and turned away. Similar to the experience of smelling marijuana, once you smell the stench of a decaying human body, it's something you never forget.

I could hear bombs and explosions going off in the distance. The smell and feel of the air were unbearable—a combination of open sewer fumes and thick exhaust clouds from trucks, cars, and motorcycles, all without mufflers.

One vision still haunts me to this day. I came across a small man. The left side of his face was missing. His remaining eyeball hung on in the middle of a mass of black, blue, and red open wounds. I saw him kneeling down on the street with a tin can in one hand and a homemade stick for a cane in the other.

I also saw people defecating on the sidewalks, living in complete squalor. These horrendous conditions remain unlike anything I've ever experienced in my life. Sure, I'd seen awful war scene images like these on the news, but when they're right in front of you, in person, it's a distinct reality that changes you forever. Images from those experiences never left me.

Every night locked in my room, I prayed the Viet Cong wouldn't attack. Each day brought new hope because I knew I was a day closer to going home. When I awoke with two days left, I thought things were looking good. One more night and I'd be on my flight back to Glenwood.

That afternoon the family and I met at the family attorney's office in a small building constructed from bamboo and scrap metal. I was instructed to sit in the front of the office while the family members and attorney held their meeting in the back of the shanty. I heard loud voices, but I didn't know what they were talking about. After an hour, the attorney came to the front of the office and smiled.

"You stay longer. We extend visa."

I felt my stomach drop.

"No, no, no. I'm leaving tomorrow on my flight. I wish I could help you, but I'm out of here tomorrow."

"I not ask you. I tell you. Family decide, you stay."

"No, sir, I only have a seven-day visa. I'd like to help, but I'm out of here tomorrow."

"No. I fix visa. Black market. No problem. Family decide, you stay."

The words of the embassy attaché yelling that if I needed help while in Vietnam, I was on my own echoed in my mind. Now I felt terrified like I'd never been before. A few minutes later, we left the office. The family had taken two cars to the office, and remembering what Yoly told me about Carol, I asked if I could ride back to the house with her.

On the drive home, I repeated what the attorney had said to confirm I understood everything. She confirmed. I was at the end of my line.

"Look, I've done everything asked of me. I signed every document. I didn't tell the embassy attaché what was going on. I've cooperated in every way possible."

"Yes, you did Jerry. Thank you."

"But the deal was I only stay here seven days and no longer. That was the agreement. The US consulate officer told me I must leave before seven days, no matter what."

"Yes. But we can fix the visa. No problem."

We drove in silence for a few more minutes. I looked out the window and took in the horrific scenes I'd been witness to over the past six days. No way in hell was I gonna stay another day in this place.

"Carol, Yoly told me you would help me if something went wrong. This is wrong. I'm going to the airport tomorrow, even if I have to walk there. Either you help me, as Yoly said you would, or I'll do it on my own."

Carol said nothing for the rest of the drive. When we pulled up to the house about thirty minutes later, she finally spoke.

"Okay. I will take you tomorrow morning to the airport. But don't tell anyone tonight. I'll make sure your bedroom door is unlocked and the lock over the bars to the stairwell isn't latched. Meet me here before sunrise."

I didn't sleep a wink that night. The next morning Carol was waiting for me as promised. She drove me to the airport. We didn't talk much, but Carol didn't seem angry. She understood my situation. When we arrived at the airport, I knew I was close to freedom. Everything back then was paper tickets and no TSA, so I had little chance of being stopped. After I made it through boarding and sat down, I closed my eyes and felt a sense of relief wash over my body. But I wasn't completely relieved in a manner I had never before experienced until the wheels to the airplane lifted off the ground. I was going home.

My seven days in Vietnam occurred in early November 1974. Five months later the North Vietnamese invaded Saigon. Corrina and Suzy made it to the US embassy with all the paperwork that had been produced during my stay. A helicopter airlifted them to US Navy ships waiting offshore.

They made their way to a refugee camp in San Diego. Yoly, working with some Iowa senators and congressmen, was able to get them out of the refugee camp to come to Glenwood. A couple of years later, Carol and her husband escaped Vietnam through the black market by becoming what was then known as "Boat People." Today, Carol lives in Council Bluffs, Iowa, and Corrina and Suzy live in Little Rock, Arkansas.

After I made it back to Glenwood, I felt guilty for a long time. I was ashamed I'd been so scared. I'd only spent seven days there and in relative safety, for the most part. I knew that thousands of soldiers had been facing enemies in rice paddies and jungles for years. I remember thinking about all the Americans who'd been killed or injured. Some of them were from my hometown. Some my family knew.

I hadn't faced that kind of danger, or seen anyone I cared for die, yet the fear I felt during that week took me years to get over. Embarrassed about how I felt, I didn't talk about what I experienced for years.

My Vietnam experience was the first of two crossroad events in my life. As terrible as it was, the wake-up call turned out to be what I needed. I realized I'd been wasting my life; something had to change. I thought back on the way I was behaving and how immature I'd been. I could've lost my freedom by making one bad mistake while under the influence of alcohol. I was arrogant to think I could scam my country, and even though I was exposed, somehow, once again, I escaped unscathed. I knew my breaks wouldn't last forever. And even if they did, that wasn't how I wanted to live my life. It was time to make a decision.

I had no direction and no education to impress any potential employer. During this period of self-reflection, I started to dream for real. That first dream wasn't vivid, but it was a dream. I knew I wanted to change and make something of my life—to become someone who didn't get breaks but made things happen in a respectable way. I thought about Karen. I dreamed of marrying her and of starting a life together. I'd spent only seven days in Vietnam, but the net effect of those seven harrowing days changed my life.

MY BROTHER LARRY

When you make an important decision, that doesn't mean things are guaranteed to work out in your favor. It just means you've given yourself a fighting chance. You might decide to start a business, and a year later you close the doors because it failed. Or maybe you decide to start a business, and it doesn't fail, but you discover you hate running the business.

The reality is we make hundreds of decisions every day. Do you wake up on time or keep hitting the snooze button? Do you go to the gym or watch another episode of the new hit show everyone is talking about? Those are small decisions, but over time they affect you in a big way.

When you face a big decision, you can see and feel the immediate risk. Starting a business is a high-risk decision. Making a career change and switching companies can be a high-risk decision. You should take time to weigh the pros and cons before making a life-changing decision. And keep in mind saying "no" is a decision too. When you make a decision, you close a loop in your mind so you can put your mental energy toward the next thing. It's the only way to move forward.

The lesson I want to emphasize here is that you can't avoid making decisions because you're afraid of failure. The more decisions you make, the better you'll get. Keep in mind, often the outcome of a decision can feel like a failure when things don't turn out the way you envisioned. However, a decision that doesn't yield the results you had in mind can still open new doors of opportunity you never would've seen without making the decision.

Upon my return home from Vietnam, I started making decisions, and life got better. I stopped drinking heavily, broke away from the bad influence crowd, and put all my focus on work and building a strong relationship with Karen. In the spring of 1976, I asked Karen to marry me, and she said yes. The wedding was set for October. I felt like my life was finally heading in the right direction. Then tragedy shattered my world.

My brother Larry was a distributor for Standard Oil and had many large fuel tanks at what he'd called "the tank farm." Part of his job was cleaning the tanks on the rare occasion they needed to be cleaned out. Typically, Larry would outsource the cleaning, but to save some money, he recruited his best friend to help him clean a large tank.

They borrowed gas masks from the National Guard facility in town because once you're in the tank's belly, the fumes require a breathing apparatus.

To clean the tanks, they had to crawl through a tiny access panel at the top of the tank and climb down a very narrow ladder. One day, soon after they'd made their way into the tank and started the cleaning process, Larry collapsed. His friend did everything he could to drag Larry out of the tank, but carrying a limp, 175-pound body up a long narrow ladder is too much to ask of anyone. After several failed efforts to get Larry out, Larry's friend rushed to a neighboring house and called 911.

It was too late by the time help arrived.

Later we discovered the gas masks were designed for chemical warfare protection, not to filter fuel fumes. We assumed the area of the tank where Larry was working contained more fumes and less air; otherwise, two people would have died that day.

The day Larry died, I was nine miles away at the Mills County Fair with Karen. A deputy sheriff found me, verified that I was Jerry Banks, and told me I needed to go home right away. Karen was showing in a horse show, and I wasn't about to leave without knowing more, so I pressed the sheriff to give me more details. Finally he said, "Your brother has died in an accident, and you need to get home."

I found Karen, relayed the news, then drove about ninety miles per hour to the family business. When I pulled in, the parking lot was full. People from town were standing outside talking. When I got out of my car, everyone stopped talking almost all at once and stared at me.

"Where's my mom and dad?" I asked.

Somebody in the crowd said they were upstairs, so I bolted to the top floor. Mom was a complete mess, and Dad was trying to console her. I asked them what happened. I don't remember who told me the story, but I remember the next day I had the difficult job of calling friends, family, and business partners to break the tragic news.

At this point, the only thing I've told you so far about my older brother Larry is that he was seven years older than me and died at age twenty-eight in a work accident. You also might remember he encouraged me to go to Vietnam to help get his wife's sisters out of the country. Okay, so that's three things.

What you don't know yet is that I don't have many positive memories about my brother Larry. What I have are many memories of him calling me a loser who would never amount to anything. Although Larry never physically abused me, his verbal abuse was relentless and cut deep throughout our upbringing together. The one phrase he repeated over and over, which stuck in my heart and mind, was, "You're a piece of shit." I know how ironic that is now, considering the title of this book, but that line always hurt the most.

My parents did very little to intervene. They knew Larry bullied me and would occasionally tell him to be nice, but their admonishment never took. They felt Larry's words were normal brotherly bantering, despite the one-sidedness of the attacks. Maybe they just didn't know what to do to stop it—and hoped it would pass. The sad truth is Larry tormented me nonstop from my earliest memories up to his passing. By the time he died, I felt nothing but anger and contempt toward him.

Larry's burial at the Glenwood Cemetery remains a vivid memory. I sat in a metal folding chair in the front row with Karen by my side, his casket a few feet away, covered in an American flag. A large crowd surrounded the family. Mom was sobbing and shaking. Yoly and Dad did their best to help her. Sheila, Larry's daughter, was three years old and didn't know what was going on.

I can still see the casket being lowered into that dark hole as a trumpet played "Taps." Karen held my hand. The dominant emotion at my brother's funeral was anger. I kept thinking, "Here I am, two months from my wedding, and now my family is discussing canceling the celebration because of Larry."

Once again, Larry had stepped on me. And worst of all, he'd never have to face the truth of what he did to me. I never got my chance to look him in the eye man to man and ask him, "Why?" Justice wouldn't be served. I would never get from him what he owed me: an apology.

I made a vow that day, sitting feet from his casket, that I would never return to his grave. You might think this sounds terrible. Well, the truth is often terrible, and it's how I felt.

After Larry's funeral, Dad decided I would operate Larry's fuel and distribution business until it could be sold. This entailed driving a large truck that contained six compartments, holding a mixture of different fuels for farms, trucking companies, and other volume fuel consumers. During the spring planting and fall harvest, I would make deliveries from six in the morning to midnight, seven days a week. In the summer, it would scale back to only sixty hours a week. I remember the resentment I felt about it and thinking what a nice way to start my new life with Karen! Thanks, big brother.

My marriage with Karen stayed on schedule, and we were married in October during the height of the harvest. One of my best friends, Greg Ross, got married a week after me to his fiancé Buffy. We'd planned a honeymoon cruise in the Caribbean. That trip never happened due to me running Larry's business. Instead, Karen and I spent two nights in Kansas City before rushing back home so I could make fuel deliveries. How romantic.

During those long days and nights alone on the truck, I started dreaming in more detail about what I wanted to do when the fuel business was sold. I even entertained the thought of buying it myself, but I wasn't sure I wanted to be in the fuel business. Thankfully, I didn't have to wrestle with the idea of buying Larry's business for long. After running the business for close to a year, one day Dad told me the business had been sold. The next day I started training the new owner. Since he was a hardworking, smart local farm kid, the training took me less than a week. He already knew about the various fuels we delivered and had connections with many of the clients.

Selling the business was a decision Dad made for me, resulting in me going back into the family real estate business in 1977 at twenty-two years old. I had fulfilled my duty to the family. Now I had an opportunity to do something for myself.

If I had the courage.

THE 5 KEYS TO PROGRAMMING GOOD DECISIONS

1. **Conduct Thorough Research:** Before meetings or making decisions, research extensively. Look into social media, Google names and businesses, and dig deep into relevant topics.

2. **Understand the Subject Matter:** For any project or transaction, know more about the subject than anyone else. For example, in real estate, you want to research zoning, ownership, neighborhood crime statistics, demographics, traffic patterns, history, and more.

3. **Question and Verify:** Don't just take someone's word. Study the topic to learn as much as possible and make practical, informed decisions that are defensible if challenged.

4. **Be Skeptical:** Be inquisitive and don't accept information blindly. Run different scenarios and see how things work to make decisions that advance you toward your dreams.

5. **Seek Advice:** Get input from as many sources as possible. Learning from those who failed at what you're about to try is valuable.

TAKE A CHANCE ON YOURSELF

Here's a hard truth. You're not always going to have cheerleaders and a stand full of fans cheering you on in life. If you're lucky, you will have some good people who support you and give you good advice, but many people won't, and that's okay.

Whether or not you like it, you're the final decision maker in the way your life story ends. If you decide not to make tough decisions, that is a decision. It's also the worst thing you can do because it'll almost certainly lead to regret. When you want to do something great in life, you will often feel like you're alone because you are. Everybody has their own problems. Dealing with your problems is hard enough. You can't depend on others to make your dreams come true.

You'll have to make decisions others disagree with or discourage you from making. Hear people out, evaluate their reasons, but if their reasons aren't in your interest, then you need to decide to take a chance on yourself. At the end of the day, whatever the outcome is will be because of you and your dedication to your dreams, your decisions, your determination, your discipline, and your resilience. Take ownership and create a life you're proud of.

The dreaming I did while driving Larry's fuel truck ended up being a gift I did not expect. Still, to this day, I do some of my best thinking and dreaming on the road. One thing that bubbled to the surface during those long hauls was the thought about who I wanted to be and how I wanted others to see me.

Two questions haunted me. If I stayed in Glenwood and kept working in the family business, I could have a good life, but would it be because of me or because of my last name and my father setting me up in the business? And worse, what if I failed? People would think I was given a head start, lots of opportunity, and I squandered it. I continually wrestled with these two questions.

Now that I was working back in the family business, more and more I wanted to get out. In the winter of 1978, my dad bought a Century 21 franchise to enhance our real estate sales operations in Glenwood. I was managing our Shenandoah, Iowa, office. I was also overseeing our Glenwood offices' salespeople, recruiting, and training.

After Dad purchased the franchise, I started taking sales and management training classes at the Century 21 office in Omaha. I still remember my first trip to the offices. As I waited in the reception room, I witnessed a fax machine operating for the first time. My small town and low-tech brain were overwhelmed. How in the hell could that small machine send a copy of a document over telephone lines? I couldn't wait to tell everyone back in Glenwood what I'd seen that day in the big city of Omaha. It seemed magical, and maybe I could bring that magic home!

Over three months, I took all the Century 21 sales training courses and found inspiration in a trainer named Steve Ruff. Steve was a crazy young instructor who often showed up late to teach his courses. He typically wore a dress shirt, tie, and that horrible mustard-colored Century 21 sport coat (my apologies to Century 21). Cutoff blue jean shorts and tennis shoes complimented his sports coat. Perhaps best of all, Steve had no shame in admitting he was late because his morning golf game ran long. I immediately took a liking to him!

In a bit of irony, Steve would become a major mortgage banker in Omaha. When I started my career in real estate investment, we reconnected and did a significant amount of business over the years. He'd grown out of the cutoff blue jean shorts by then. He and I remain friends to this day and often laugh about our Century 21 days. But at the time, Steve encouraged me. Often he'd tell me I had what it took to own and operate my own Century 21 business. Over time I began to believe him and started positioning myself to do just that.

I finally felt like I was heading in the right direction. I knew I had to get out of Glenwood, and owning a franchise was my ticket. But I was conflicted with doubt. Could I do it? How would I do it? Was I making a mistake? Even more, I was on my own because I didn't tell Dad my plans. I was worried he might be mad at me for leaving the family business.

But I'd made my decision, so I started looking around for a Century 21 franchise outside of Glenwood that I could purchase. After about six months, I received a call from the regional VP of Century 21. He said the existing Century 21 office in Council Bluffs might be for sale and gave me the owner's name and phone number.

On Thursday, November 1, 1979, I closed on my acquisition of that Century 21 office. I was twenty-four years old and pretty sure I knew everything there was to know about real estate and real estate broker-age. At least that's what my cocky self thought.

By this time, Karen was eight months pregnant with our daughter Kelley. It took $20,000 to purchase what was essentially a franchise name, a bunch of used office equipment, and a big pile of "For Sale" signs. My challenge was to convince the four existing agents to stay with me, along with their property listings. One of those four agents was Jim Kaiser. Jim stayed on and helped me in so many ways. He gave me his perspective on the market, people, and selling real estate in Council Bluffs.

Jim is still active in Council Bluffs real estate, and we remain good friends. I'll never forget that about a year after purchasing the company, Jim came into my office and proudly held out his hand for a handshake. He said he wanted to thank me for buying the company and helping him. He told me he had doubled his income under my ownership. While his words humbled me, in the back of my head I was thinking to myself, "But Jim, you hardly made anything this last year."

After he left my office, I quickly opened the files (we didn't have computers back then) and looked up his 1980 earnings. He'd made about $7,000. That meant he'd made $3,500 the year before! And yet he was happy. I thought to myself, "I'm so screwed if one of my better agents is happy making $7,000 a year. How will he, I, or this company survive?"

To acquire Century 21 in Council Bluffs, I put in $10,000 in cash, which represented my life savings to that point. I borrowed $20,000 on a second mortgage against our house. This gave me $10,000 of extra operating cash after paying $20,000 to the seller. After the sale, I was deeply leveraged. One thing I didn't factor in was that Ronald Reagan had beaten Jimmy Carter in the presidential election. President Reagan made it known that he backed Federal Reserve Chairman Paul Volcker and that interest rates would go up.

Just before closing, I asked my banker what he thought about the increasing interest rates. I told him I could still cancel my purchase and that I was worried about what would happen to real estate sales if interest rates stayed high or went higher. He told me not to worry as interest rates would be down by spring. I proceeded with the purchase. He was correct. Interest rates fell in the spring. Unfortunately, it was six years later in the spring of 1986!

The biggest lesson I learned in Vietnam was that I had to choose to take control of my life. Nobody was going to do it for me. That led to deciding to clean up my lifestyle, get serious about my relationships, and start something new for myself. It was the right decision, but life had other things in store for me with the passing of my brother. But even that forced me to dig deeper and dream with more clarity.

Wherever you are in life, it's important to know that your situation can change for better or worse, and it may be completely out of your control. Keep dreaming, and when you have the opportunity to act and make a decision to correct your course, take advantage of it. Having the will and courage to make a decision will get you closer to making your dreams come true.

Take a chance on yourself.

YOUR GPS INPUT CHECKLIST

- Make a decision, even when you're unsure of the outcome.
- Not making a decision is a decision to stay where you are.
- Decisions that don't work in your favor open new doors of opportunity.
- You're the final decision maker in your life's story.
- Have the courage to take a chance on yourself.

CHAPTER 4

ALWAYS PUT RELATIONSHIPS FIRST

"The best way to find out if you can trust somebody is to trust them."

—Ernest Hemingway

GOOD PEOPLE TELL YOU WHAT YOU NEED TO HEAR

When you go off course, there's nothing more valuable than having good people in your corner who will tell you the truth. Relationships in life and business are everything. I don't care if you work for a small company, a large corporation, or are self-employed—you can't achieve success and happiness in life without interacting with good people. Surrounding yourself with high-quality people will get you to your destination faster and expedite your recovery when things go wrong.

You have at least three different levels of relationships in your life, and they all play a critical role in your journey. Level one includes the people closest to you: your significant other, children, parents, and extended family. Level two includes your close friends, both inside and outside of the workplace. Level three includes your colleagues, vendors, and people who help you reach your goals in a more practical sense. Your accountant, banker, and lawyer may be level three, although they can also often fall into level two if the relationship survives and grows.

We're a social species. We rely on each other in more ways than we realize. In the wild, lone wolves don't survive well if they don't find a mate and create a new wolf pack of their own. It's similar for us. Knowing that relationships are invaluable to your success and an unavoidable variable in life, the smart thing to do is cultivate them by building the best relationships possible on every level. Also keep in mind that the cornerstone of every healthy relationship is trust. When I say, "Build relationships," what I'm really urging you to do is build trust with people. In reality, the strongest relationships you'll build will happen over years and decades. Developing and valuing relationships with people in your life is a long game, but nothing pays off more for your bank account and your soul.

For as long as I can recall, I've said and lived by the expression that "a true friend tells you what you need to hear, not what you want to hear." I've done my best to give those in my life license to tell me what I need to hear. I sometimes have to add, "The truth wasn't made to be nice—it was only made to be the truth, nice or not."

I learned a lot about relationships after I bought the Century 21 franchise in Council Bluffs at twenty-four. My timing wasn't ideal. Karen was eight months pregnant. I'd borrowed $20,000 on a second mortgage against our house to finance the business. That transaction happened about three months before interest rates climbed to 21 percent under Treasury Secretary Paul Volcker and President Ronald Reagan. The country plunged into a deep recession, and things only got worse from there.

Three and half years later, interest rates were still sky high. I couldn't see the light at the end of the tunnel. I was exhausted and empty. To this point, we'd been able to survive and grow the agency's sales volume, but the business wasn't profitable. I needed at least another $10,000 just to keep the lights on and pay past-due bills. I'd been working eighty-hour weeks since buying the business. My daughter Kelley was now four years old, and Karen was pregnant with our second child and working full time. I was frustrated, mad, and at my wit's end. I had no ideas left, good or bad!

One day it all came to a boiling point. I jumped in the car and drove to the First National Bank of Council Bluffs and sat in the lobby waiting to see the president of the bank, Stan Duysen. I'd known Stan since high school. He and my father had done business over the years, and we didn't have just a banking relationship. He was also like a mentor to me.

It felt like an eternity as I sat there wrestling with what I was going to say. I didn't have a definitive plan. Was I going to beg for more money? More debt would buy me more time, but as things stood, I wasn't sure if I'd ever pay the debt off. The thought of filing for bankruptcy had crossed my mind, but all my life, my parents had vilified people who had taken bankruptcy. Walking away from friends and colleagues who'd invested in me didn't seem like an option.

Mr. Duysen's secretary startled me out of my anxious thoughts.

"Mr. Banks, come with me. Mr. Duysen can see you now."

As we walked toward his office, I had my hand in my pocket fumbling with the keys to my car, home, office, desk, and file cabinets all on one gigantic key ring. After pulling the keys from my pocket, I gripped them so tight my knuckles turned white.

Stan Duysen's boisterous greeting made me even more anxious.

"Jerry Banks, the real estate king of Council Bluffs! To what do I owe this honor?" Stan was small in stature at about five feet seven inches, but his booming voice gave him a large and impressive presence. I shook his hand and forced a smile, wanting to turn and run when he called me the king of Council Bluffs real estate.

"What can I do for you?"

I didn't know what to say, so I spilled my guts.

"Mr. Duysen, I'm very sorry to do this, but I give up. I'm broke. I've done all I know how to do, but I can't generate the cash flow to pay the bills. I started out owing you $20,000 almost four years ago, and now I owe over $65,000. I have another $15,000 in past-due bills, and the electric company is about to shut off our lights."

I removed my car and house keys from the ring and threw the remaining office keys on his desk.

"I quit! Here are the keys. I'm sorry." I hadn't planned any of this, and I had no idea where my defeated reaction came from in that moment. What happened next, I'll never forget. Mr. Duysen stood up from his desk, and his whole head turned bright red. Leaning over his desk, he put his face about six inches from my nose.

"Banks! You little son of a bitch! Don't you come in here whining to me about your debt and how tired you are. Don't you dare tell me you quit. I believed in you four years ago, and I believe in you now. I have bigger loans out to kids coming out of college with just a fucking piece of paper to show for it. They don't have a business; they don't have half the experience or ability that you do. Quit feeling sorry for yourself right this second."

Then he picked my keys up off his desk and drilled me in my chest like an ace pitcher throwing a fastball.

"How much money do you need?"

"$10,000 to $15,000," I mumbled.

"Dammit, it Banks! Pick your chin up and give me a number!"

"$15,000."

He turned and yelled out the door to his secretary. "Jane, go get me a check made out to Jerry Banks for $20,000 and add it to his loan."

Turning back to me, he put his finger in my face.

"Never walk into this office again feeling sorry for yourself and throwing keys on my desk. I don't make loans to quitters or losers. And Jerry—you're not a loser, and you're not quitting. Now get your ass out of here and get to work."

I don't remember much else that happened after that because I was in shock. A few days later, Stan Duysen called me as a friend.

He didn't ask how business was going or how my cash flow was. He asked me about my attitude, my wife, my daughter, and if we were all okay. Stan cared about us as people. We weren't just another loan number to him. I later realized my professional and personal relationship with Stan saved me that day.

Within three years of that epic ass-chewing, I grew the business to thirty-six full-time agents. Our company boasted the number one market share in Southwest Iowa. We became one of the highest volume Century 21 companies in the nation, and I paid off all my loans in full.

What I needed that day was Stan Duysen's honest rant. He ignited a fire in my belly that had been burning on low and had almost gone out when I walked in his office that day. Stan was wise enough to know he needed to throw some gas on my flickering flame. Years later I realized the power and genius of Stan telling me what I needed to hear, not what I wanted to hear. He exposed me and gave me the harsh truth, but then he took steps to help me recover. I had experienced what an excellent mentor can do for someone: challenge you and get in your face. Honor those relationships. Don't reject the people who tell you straight up what you need to hear. Stan had the courage to chew me out. Too often people are so concerned about being liked, they fail to muster the courage to be honest and forthright.

Part of my hope in your journey is to help you avoid giving up like I almost did. I'm here to offer you constructive steps to prevent those feelings or to deal with them powerfully when they're building inside you. I also recommend you don't throw the keys on your banker's desk!

Throughout my own journey, I've been fortunate that people have given me a break sometimes when maybe I didn't deserve it. Looking back, these are the people who believed in me, the family members who stood by me, and many friends who lifted me up during tough times.

The value of honest relationships is an important input to program into your internal GPS. Mr. Duysen showed me the critical value of making decisions based on what's in the best interest of a relationship. To him, our relationship was key to the loan being repaid. He wouldn't have given it to me if he didn't have confidence in my ability to pay it off. In other words, his decision was based on what he knew about me and our relationship versus whatever the numbers were telling him.

How does that play out in real life when making decisions? Let's say you're working with a vendor. How do you put the relationship first? For me, I seek to be honest and open with my vendors. I always pay them on time. I affirm them when it's appropriate. I do my best to make it easy for them to do business with me and vice versa.

Building trust with everyone you do business with has a ripple effect across your career. When you cultivate relationships on a solid foundation of integrity, your good reputation will grow with you in the business community. What people you've done business with say about you creates more value for your reputation than any effort you might make through self-promotion. Sure, it doesn't hurt to go on LinkedIn, Facebook, Instagram, and other forms of social media to tell the world how great you are. It's expected. But the biggest impact on your bottom line (and your future) will result from how vendors, employees, competitors, bankers, and friends regard you and what they tell other people about you.

I keep this same mentality when I'm representing a real estate client to buy or sell something. It's my role to work with them in a mutually beneficial way. I'm making decisions based not just on what's best for me to collect a consulting fee or make a deal, but what's in the client's best interest. Sometimes that means encouraging a client to walk away from a deal. Sometimes it's even meant giving them information that will hurt the transaction and kill my fees or opportunity. My decisions are always based on the best interest of the relationship with my client. That's what pays off in the long run.

Always has been, always will be.

BUILDING TRUST

If you don't have trust, you have nothing to sell and nothing to offer. I don't care what business you're in. If your customers, vendors, and employees don't trust you, then you're on the fast track to failure. You just don't know it yet.

One of my go-to self-talk reminders is, "You have to be worthy of trust. Am I worthy of being trusted?" I want people to trust that I will be honest, candid, and not hide or take advantage of information I have access to.

Here's a secret that many people miss. To gain somebody's trust, trust them first. You must fuel their trust by first giving trust. I observe many people today, especially in business, who are secretive and try to get information without sharing it. That's backward! I'm not saying you must give away trade secrets, but the more somebody is open with me, the more comfortable I feel being open with them. It's relationship common sense. To be worthy of trust, I need to give trust too. It's a back-and-forth dynamic. You might say, "This sounds good, Jerry, but it's more complex than that!" Okay, you're right, so let me tell you how I've learned to build trust using what I call "The 5 Steps to Build Trust."

THE 5 STEPS TO BUILD TRUST

1. Start with spit and whittle.
2. Share your goals.
3. Identify any conflict.
4. Create a plan.
5. Execute the plan.

STEP 1: START WITH SPIT AND WHITTLE

Step 1 of the five-step process is what I call "start with spit and whittle." Imagine an older person, let's call him "Jim," sitting on the front porch of a country home as he whittles on a stick and turns to spit occasionally. A salesperson, let's call her "Daisy," comes up to Jim and attempts to sell him something. If Daisy immediately starts into her sales pitch, it's going nowhere. But Daisy's a good salesperson, so she sits down, embraces the setting where Jim is whittling and spitting, and starts talking about the weather or anything other than what she wants to sell Jim. Taking the time to get acquainted with a person shows you're not just interested in the sale; you're interested in the relationship you're building with that person. Every new relationship should start with spit and whittle. Let that image stick in your mind!

STEP 2: SHARE YOUR GOALS

With Step 2, I want to hear what your goals are, and I want to share my goals with you. Not sharing goals is where a lot of people go wrong. They'll talk about their goals without finding out the other person's goals, or they'll skip sharing their own. It has to be a two-way street when you share goals. In a real estate transaction, I like to share my goals up front. For example, I want to make a commission by helping you sell your property, or I might want to buy your property as an investment.

STEP 3: IDENTIFY CONFLICT

Now that you know each other's goals, for Step 3, I recommend identifying any conflict between your goals. For instance, my goal might be to buy your property. Your goal might be to never sell it and give it to your grandkids. That's a conflict. Your goal might also be to never pay a commission. My goal is to make a commission. We've just identified a conflict. Now that we've recognized the conflict, we can have an honest conversation so there's a much better chance to overcome it.

STEP 4: CREATE A PLAN

Step 4 entails creating a plan. Every plan depends on your circumstances, but by first building relational trust, sharing goals, and identifying conflict, you've built the foundation to develop a solid plan. Any good plan will outline the actions you'll take to get to the outcome each person wants. That's why it's best to create your plan with the other person if possible. If not, give them a chance to review the plan and modify it. Both parties must take ownership of the plan.

STEP 5: EXECUTE THE PLAN

Step 5 is the easiest of them all when you complete and then check off the first four steps correctly. That's executing the plan. It's just doing what you agreed to in the plan. The only thing that can mess this up is if you deviate from the plan without first discussing it with the other person.

I've discovered the importance of these five steps in any relationship. Allow me to warn you that leaving one step out, or changing the order, increases the odds of failure exponentially.

"IS IT ME?" CHECKLIST

"It's not you; it's me."

I assume you've heard that slick line before, typically in a romantic breakup when the person breaking up doesn't actually want to take responsibility for ending the relationship. Instead they pretend to be responsible ("It not you; it's me"), usually to avoid conflict or feeling too bad about themselves for breaking someone's heart.

When I'm building trust with someone and things don't go my way, I've found that more often than not, it really is me who's the problem, so I've developed a relationship exercise using a series of questions I call the "Is It Me?" Checklist. This checklist helps me evaluate whether I'm the actual cause of the problem or not and what to do about it. If I work through this exercise right, and the relationship still doesn't work out, then I know it's not me, and I can move on knowing I did my part to make it work.

"IS IT ME?" CHECKLIST

- Am I being easy to work with? If not, why not, and what do I need to change?
- Am I being easy to work for? If not, why not, and what do I need to change?
- Am I being transparent and honest? If not, why not, and what do I need to change?
- Am I being worthy of trust? If not, why not, and what do I need to change?
- Am I being courageous enough to push back in a healthy way or to be honest with criticism? If not, why not, and what do I need to change?
- Am I being too confident in my demeanor to encourage dialogue? If so, why and what do I need to change?
- Am I being genuine? If not, why not, and what do I need to change?
- Am I being somebody whom they feel they can talk to openly, candidly, and honestly? If not, why not, and what do I need to change?

When I add those questions into my internal GPS, it can guide me to do the right thing in all kinds of relationships. When I value and honor each relationship, it manifests itself in multiple ways. For example, I mentor young brokers to quit worrying about commissions and deals. I tell them to focus solely on what's in the best interest of the long-term relationship with their client. If they can make that mindset shift from focusing on what *they* want to focusing on what *their client* wants, they can transition from having a short-term job to having a long-term career.

The same values also work at home with your kids and your partner. Planning what you're going to do on vacation might not seem that important in the grand scheme of things, but when more than one person is involved, doing what's in the best interest of family relationships always pays off. If you model that process for your kids in joint decision-making, it serves everyone for years, decades, and, dare I say, a lifetime to come.

Collaboration and compromise are vital in every kind of relationship in your life. Some people have powerful personalities and are very confident. If you're like me, in some situations your own self-confidence can come off as intimidating. I'll never forget being told, for example, that I was intimidating to one of my staff members. I couldn't believe it! I never stood over his desk pointing fingers and yelling or insisting it was my way or the highway. Me? Intimidating? They had to be wrong. Then I was forced to see how my self-confidence intimidated the individual who reported to me. He lacked the self-confidence to debate or argue with me.

What a wake-up call.

After that, I made a conscious effort to change my method of communicating, not just with him but with everyone. I worked at telling everyone how I enjoy debate while also communicating my need for feedback about things like property operations, staffing, management companies, acquisitions, or financing. I even did my best to give every-one a license or permission to debate and argue with me without consequences.

I adopted the belief and phrase that good decisions come from open and honest debate and told people about it. Obviously, at the end of the day, someone needs to make a decision, but to make good deci-sions, you need information. Allowing yourself to be open to opinions that are contrary to yours helps you make good decisions.

I would also often try to add a bit of levity to this process by saying something like, "It pains me to say this, but you're right," or "it pains me to admit your idea was better than mine." Adding a little humor to what can feel like a moment of tension goes a long way in letting the other person know you are genuine and there are no hard feelings. To be honest, I still have to work at healthy relationship building, and I'm not ashamed to admit it's not the easiest thing for me to do!

YOUR GPS INPUT CHECKLIST

- Good people tell you what you need to hear.
- Cultivate relationships in your life at every level.
- Without trust, you have nothing to sell and nothing to offer.
- To get somebody's trust, you have to trust them first.
- Check if you've done your part to make a relationship work before moving on.

CHAPTER 5

SUCCESS TAKES DISCIPLINE

*"If you are not willing to learn, no one can help you.
If you are determined to learn, no one can stop you."*

—Zig Ziglar

CULTIVATE A STRONG TEAM

Success takes discipline, but when you make it a team effort, amazing things can happen. By building a resilient team and strong culture, your business can endure the storms. Sometimes the only way to find out who your strong players are is by going through a battle together. You quickly find out who's invested in seeing the operation succeed, and who's just punching the clock.

When you're running a lean operation, you can't have clock punchers—at least not in the important positions. And when you're at the helm, and the team is looking to you to survive another day, you must lead by example. For me, that meant making sure I was putting the time and effort to at least the same level, and often more so, than many of my team members. I wouldn't check out at noon on Friday to play golf and ask them to get the work done. Obviously, not always, but on many days, my office light would be the last to be turned off at the end of the day. Staff members also realized when they came in on a Monday morning that I had been at the office over the weekend because they'd find memos or notes on their desk from me that weren't there when they left on Friday night.

You might not start with the best team, but success attracts success. Finding ways to motivate, encourage, and get the best out of everyone builds strong teams. Over time momentum builds, and people see what you're doing and want to be part of it. That's how you attract more talent.

When you're starting out, you need people who are hungry or, as I like to say, people who have fire in their bellies. They might not have the most talent, but fire in their bellies can make up for that in spades. Create a vision together, one that has stakes for everyone. Go all in on helping your employees and teammates reach their goals.

One of my tricks is using the Pygmalion effect—a psychological phenomenon in which you give someone high expectations, which leads to improved performances. Conversely, low expectations lead to worse performances. I do my best to have high expectations of everyone around me, and when I let them know what I expect, I've found that 99 percent of the time they live up to those expectations.

The launch of Century 21 Banks Realty led me to some amazing people who taught me tons about selling, real estate, and more about life. The agents who stayed helped me survive and grow. They had fire in their bellies. Our gang went through both tough and great times together. Nothing brings a team together like operating out of a foxhole.

We were fighting a common enemy during those early years: a shaky market. Every sale felt like a hard-won battle. Our competition was well established, and our primary competitor had been the number one company in real estate sales in the area for several years.

It wasn't always easy, and there were times when I didn't feel like we would make it. The turns, curves, spins, highs, and lows of the roller coaster were many and often.

I'd often work Sunday night in the office by myself, trying to get my arms around the business. By the end of the evening, I was depressed, stressed, or often both. I didn't see a light at the end of the tunnel. One thing that kept me going was the Monday morning sales meetings where my agents reported multiple sales, new listings, and activity. On those days I'd be on top of the world, but the reality is each week felt like it was up in the air, and we were barely hanging on.

Through hard work and discipline, we were able to recruit the best agents, train them, market our listings faster, and surpass our competitors. After a few years of hanging on, we won many awards from Century 21 for our volume. We were recognized as one of the top producing offices in the Century 21 system. People such as Bud Mahan, Frankie Watkins, Jim Kaiser, Steve Riso, Carol Duggan, Louise Anderson, Jim McPartland, Bill and Judy Smith, Ginny Lepley, Mike Fox, Judy Ernst (known to us as Precious), Dan Van Houten, Steve Johnson, Randall Haines, Al Smith, and many, many more worked on our team.

At our peak, we were processing over 600 transactions a year, and this was back when the agents and broker had to transact every bit of the closing. There weren't escrow agents or closing agents. I personally approved every closing statement and signed every check on all transactions.

Our success was a result of several factors. First off, the agents who stayed on wanted change. The previous owner had a poor reputation in the real estate market, and they were happy to see him go and for me to come in. Almost immediately I learned that one agent who planned on leaving was Bud Mahan and that if I could convince him to stay, it would be a huge win for the company.

The key to the residential real estate business is having the best agents. It's about recruiting the best people. Bud was one of the most respected real estate agents in town and a top producer. I knew we needed Bud, so I gave everything I had to get him to stay. I spent hours with him, finding out what was important to him. I told him about my dream, my passion for the company, my background, and my desire to build a company with full-time, professional agents.

Over a fast and furious two-week period, Bud and I developed a strong relationship. He could see that I was driven and was willing to go all in on helping him achieve his dreams. It was a major coup when Bud decided to stay with me instead of moving to a different company as he'd originally planned.

Over the years, Bud helped me recruit other agents. His reputation and influence made a huge difference. Bud had a big impact on me personally. His mentoring and friendship remain within me to this day, and for that, I will always be eternally grateful.

The early eighties were a very tough period for the residential real estate sector. Interest rates for new home loans ran from 10 to 15 percent. Real estate brokerage companies were closing shop left and right. People were getting out of the business and going to anything that had a steady paycheck. The only people staying in the business were the best of the best.

As this was taking place, I did everything I could to identify strong agents at other companies in Council Bluffs and started building relationships with them. I'd tell them about the benefits of being in the Century 21 system and the benefits of joining our company. We were all full-time agents dedicated to being first-class professionals. When you worked with us, you were working with the best of the best.

Then (and to a degree today) real estate agents had a bad rap as being sleazy. We wanted to do it differently and change the narrative, so we dressed and acted like professionals at all times. I wouldn't put up with anyone working under our flag being dishonest with our clients or even our competitors. Ethics wasn't just discussed; it was a nonnegotiable value within our company. Reputation was everything.

As other companies in Council Bluffs folded, we'd recruit and pick off maybe one or two of their very best. Momentum built, and we transitioned some agents over from other companies as well. Two agents I'll never forget are Bill and Judy Smith.

Judy Smith worked for Better Homes and Gardens. Her husband Bill worked for me at Century 21. He was successful, while Judy floundered at Better Homes and Gardens. Bill wanted her to switch companies, but she loved her fellow agents and felt loyal to the owners. She'd been with them for almost two years, but she was making beans compared to what Bill was clearing working for me.

At Bill's encouragement, I started meeting with Judy regularly, and after months of wooing her, she finally made the switch. As she got settled into our company, I asked Judy if I could accompany her on some appointments. It didn't take long for me to realize that Judy knew her facts about real estate. She had the knowledge and information to answer every question buyers or sellers had. Technically, she was sharp as they come. Her only problem was she lacked self-confidence. She'd never ask for the order. She'd convince herself the client would say no before she gave them a chance to say anything at all.

Once I realized this, I started working with her on some techniques and primarily told her she had what it took and to buck up and ask for the order. She listened, and the rest is history. All she needed was someone to spend one-on-one time with her in observation, then to support her. Within six months of joining our company, she started building a business that led to her becoming one of the upper tier salespeople in the company every year.

What brought me the most satisfaction is the year she beat Bill in sales volume. That was so cool, and Bill was immensely proud of her. In 1987, when I sold Century 21, Bill and Judy bought the company from me. I couldn't have handed it off to better stewards.

Some agents who joined me in this venture introduced me to the writings (and tapes) of people such as Zig Ziglar, Og Mandino, Norman Vincent Peale, and Dr. Maxwell Maltz. I read their books and listened to their tapes over and over and over. They had a huge impact on me in that season and my life going forward. I still display books by Zig Ziglar and Og Mandino on my bookshelves. I often give them to graduates and people I mentor.

Those brilliant thinkers helped me take my habit of dreaming and gave it purpose. Their motivation put my dreaming on steroids. They gave me words, explanations, and guidance to something I deeply felt but was still learning to apply to my journey.

Zig Ziglar introduced me to the world of possibility thinking in his amazing book *See You at the Top*. Og Mandino's *The Greatest Salesman in the World* gave me the words and determination to adopt the mantra, "I will persist until I succeed."

Through these books and tapes, I realized my dreaming wasn't silly or a waste of time. My hope is my recommendations in this book will help light a fire in your belly.

THE 5 KEYS TO TEAM ENGAGEMENT

1. **Encourage Open Dialogue:** Create an environment where all team members feel comfortable sharing their ideas, regardless of their position or the perceived feasibility of their suggestions. Emphasize that there are no bad ideas, as even the most unconventional thoughts can lead to valuable insights.

2. **Address Employee Dissatisfaction:** Recognize that feeling undervalued or ignored can lead to employee dissatisfaction and turnover. Regularly check in with your team to ensure they feel respected and listened to.

3. **Personalize Your Approach:** Take the time to get to know your team members on a personal level. Addressing them by their first names and showing interest in their lives outside of work can strengthen their sense of belonging and loyalty to the team.

4. **Foster a Sense of Family and Teamwork:** Cultivate an atmosphere of teamwork and family. This can be achieved by celebrating successes together, supporting each other through challenges, and fostering a sense of camaraderie among team members.

5. **Exercise the Pygmalion Effect:** Have high expectations of everyone around you.

KEEP EXPANDING YOUR SKILL SET

Keep expanding your skills, even when you're experiencing success. The worst thing you can do when things are going well in business is get complacent. Sometimes I find myself curious about a subject that seems as though it has nothing to do with my dream, my business, or today's problems. Despite that, I'll research and learn about it to resolve my curiosity. I can't tell you how many times, months later, something has come up related to the subject.

A great example of this played out for me during my years running Century 21 Banks Realty. I continually searched for education opportunities, and through the National Association of Realtors, I discovered the Realtors National Marketing Institute (RNMI). RNMI offered specialized seminars related to real estate. I started with a series of courses about real estate brokerage management. I took all the required courses in brokerage management and received the professional designation referred to as the Certified Real Estate Brokerage Manager (CRB). Then I learned about a series of courses leading to the Certified Commercial Investment Member (CCIM) designation. I took the first of the five-course series in Kansas City in 1983. That first course helped ignite a fire in me for commercial investment real estate.

The course was incredibly intense and went Monday through Friday from 8:00 a.m. until 5:00 p.m. We had a one-hour break.

Then a group-style homework session started at 6:00 p.m. and lasted as late as we wanted to go. Most of us would hit the mental wall between 9:00 p.m. and 10:00 p.m. and tap out for the night. All of this was building toward a final exam on Saturday morning. The exam was twenty-five questions, and you could only miss three questions or fewer to pass. It took me over three hours to complete the exam. I didn't ace it, but I think I only missed two or three and passed.

Over the next three years I continued the CCIM series and took all the additional courses. To obtain the designation, I would be required to provide a demonstration report or case study, a resume of commercial activity, and be interviewed by a panel of experts. I never earned the CCIM designation because I was more interested in the value of the education than the designation itself. At the time, I was transitioning into the pizza business and became blinded by its early success. I wasn't even sure I would continue in the real estate world.

After my experience with the CCIM, I found out about some intensive courses in Chicago the Securities and Syndication Institute offered. I was interested in two courses on the syndication of real estate investments, but they were limited to thirty participants. I applied for both and was accepted.

The first was primarily on the structure of partnerships and the legal requirements for raising capital from investors. The second course, my favorite, took what I had learned in the CCIM courses and not only put them into real-world cases, but put them on steroids. We learned about tax law and structuring ideas that could enhance returns on potential investments. The last two days of the course, we were divided into groups of four and given a sample investment case. Each group had to structure and present a case for acquiring the subject investment property, with scenarios of creative ideas used to enhance the returns for your investors.

The ideas and concepts presented in those two days applied creativity to investments in ways I'd never imagined possible. Every group had different and unique ideas that I'd never been exposed to. Through this series of courses, I determined what I wanted my life course to be and started dreaming again. I wanted to transition into the commercial real estate investment business, but I would have never been exposed to this opportunity if I didn't have the discipline to keep expanding my skill sets.

Soon after taking the courses in Chicago, I met a very interesting man named Dr. Hansmann who lived in Council Bluffs. He'd emigrated from Germany and brought with him a heavy accent. He and his wife were in their seventies when I met them, and he was still working full time. Dr. Hansmann wanted to invest in small apartment properties such as an eight-plex. He ended up becoming my first client in the investment world. Dr. Hansmann always encouraged me to pursue more education and a career in investment real estate. We became good friends and remained so until his death in 1990.

The years of coursework I went through gave me the skills I would use later in my career, and all the hard work paid off. It was a grind, to say the least, but the determination and discipline to see it through, no matter what, got me closer to achieving my new dream of a successful career in commercial real estate.

DRAW FROM YOUR BUCKET OF BLESSINGS

One of my strengths (and sometimes a weakness) is my complete honesty. The truth is you'll hit discouraging detours and setbacks on your path toward your dreams. When this happens, the easy thing to do is give up. During moments of adversity, the negative voices in your head start talking:

"I told you this wasn't going to work."

"Dad, mom, brother, sister, friend was right. I'm not cut out for this."

"Better to cut my losses now and do something with less risk."

"My brother was right—I am a piece of shit."

As loud and discouraging as these voices are, I promise setbacks are a valuable part of the journey to achieving your dreams.

FAILURE IS NOT THE OPPOSITE OF SUCCESS

You'll hear me say failure is not the opposite of success. It's a necessary step that leads to your success, and I'll say that more than once as you read on. It's also critical to get that idea into your internal GPS. If setbacks are inevitable, the best thing you can do is know they're coming and have a plan to face them when they arrive. A great life hack I've learned to keep me encouraged when I hit bumps in my journey is being grateful for my "bucket of blessings." Gratitude is one key to living the "eat shit and smile" philosophy of life.

Most of us have a bucket list of things we hope to someday experience. More important is to have a bucket of blessings to draw and reflect upon. It's a metaphorical bucket full of blessings you've identified in your life. These are the things that cause you to overflow with gratitude when you stop and reflect on them. My bucket of blessings is where I've learned to go when I need something to sustain me through tough times. I go there when my emotional energy flatlines. I use it to recharge my life battery.

One of the strengths of ambitious people is always looking ahead toward their next goal. However, this mentality can be a double-edged sword when things go off track. For highly driven people, setbacks feel like personal failures, and the big ones can quickly spiral out of control. Only when you step aside and reflect on your journey as a whole can you gain perspective and see whatever problem you're facing now isn't the end of the road.

My bucket of blessings includes an incredible family. I have two amazing daughters who have husbands I'm proud to call my sons-in-law. Their respective families have helped fill my bucket of blessings with seven respectful, smart grandchildren whom I dearly love and can't spend enough time with.

My bucket of blessings is filled with great memories of friends, trips, and life experiences. Inside my bucket, I can find the names, faces, and memories of some incredible relationships I have had with coworkers, employers, partners, vendors, and more. Some blessings have been brought by financial rewards that have occurred beyond my expectations.

With maturity and reflection, I've continued to add to my bucket the hardships, failures, and pain of the setbacks I've endured. For they, perhaps more than the successes, molded me in ways that today I'm incredibly thankful for.

When you're in a good place in life, take the time to identify who and what is in your bucket of blessings. Write them down so you can find them when you need to. Your bucket of blessings will surely be different from mine, especially if you're not a parent or grandparent. If you take the time to travel backward on your journey, you will find some amazing blessings you can feel proud of that give you perspective. If you're young, it could be graduating from college or getting your certification in something that advances your career. It may be a partner or a loved one.

Another thing I would think about when I was facing hard times was the fact that I live in the United States of America. What a blessing! What if I was stuck in a country dealing with war and poverty like Vietnam when I went there? As a United States citizen, you have protection and opportunities not afforded to so many outside this country. I always remind myself that no matter how bad things get, I'll be okay because I live in the greatest country the world has ever known.

HOLD YOUR GROUND WHEN THE STORMS COME

Somewhere along the line, I heard or read a philosophy that I liked and adopted. The philosophy is there's a limit to how many noes you'll receive in selling. The sooner you get through the noes, the sooner you'll arrive at the yeses. I adopted this philosophy to counter negatives in life. I'd often think to myself that whatever negative I was going through, it was good to get it out of the way and bring me closer to the positives.

I also realized I would just as soon have all these negatives occur earlier in life so that later in life it would be the proverbial bed of roses. As I reflect upon my life, it seems this is true. Not that I don't have problems or issues today, but in terms of magnitude, they don't compare. I guess this is what many call paying your dues. I paid a lot of dues, and I'm thankful I did. Trust me, you will too!

Not all storms come to reap destruction. Some come to clear your path. When in the path of the storm, or in the center of the tornado, it's extremely difficult to remember this. Have faith in the process. Close your eyes, dream, believe, and stay true to the course. Don't take shortcuts. Often when our backs are against the wall, we start with little lies and a little cheating, and moral weakness starts creeping in. It's easy to start playing the blame game. It's much easier to point your finger than take responsibility.

I promise that if you stay the course and absorb the negatives with strong moral character, it will pay dividends. Accept responsibility and reflect on what you could have done better or differently. Allow the mess and the process to teach you and not beat you.

I recall a banker friend of mine telling me about two brothers who had jointly borrowed money from him. I knew both Mark and Jim. Mark had a reputation for being a pretty classy guy and sharp dresser with the personality of a savvy businessman. Jim was the polar opposite—a party guy, a heavy drinker, often in bar fights, and dressed like he just walked off the back forty acres after feeding the hogs. Over time Mark and Jim's business ran into trouble, so they stopped making their loan payments.

The banker told me he would never loan money to Mark again. However, he might loan money to Jim under the right circumstances. I was surprised and asked him why Jim and not Mark?

"You can tell more about a person when their back is against the wall than you can when things are going great," the banker told me. Apparently, when this banker was going through the loan collection efforts, Mark went into hiding and wouldn't return his phone calls. Jim, on the other hand, returned every phone call and was always transparent and honest about what was going on.

People will remember and tell others how you acted when your back was against the wall. Make it so they can talk about you in a positive light despite the storms you're trying to survive.

YOUR GPS INPUT CHECKLIST

- A team member with fire in their belly can often trump talent.
- Expand your skills, even when you're experiencing success.
- Failure is not the opposite of success. It's a necessary step along the path to success.
- Draw from your bucket of blessings to sustain yourself through hard times.
- You can tell more about a person when their back is against the wall than you can when things are going great.

CHAPTER 6

TURN BAD DECISIONS INTO LESSONS

"I never lose. I either win or learn."

—Nelson Mandela

ALMOST BANKRUPT AGAIN

Here's a critical point to put into your internal GPS: You must accept responsibility for your own future and destiny. Sometimes things happen out of your control that can change dreams and plans. You deal with those as they happen.

Sometimes things just don't work out, no matter how much planning you do. One bad decision or a changing wind can throw you off what you thought was the right course. It's during those times that you must stay determined to make the best of a difficult situation, cut your losses, reflect on what you learned, and trust that new opportunities lie ahead. It is also good to remember that calm weather teaches the sea captain very little. Sea captains learn the most from the storms they endure.

I had a significant life storm detour me from my dream in 1985 when I ventured into the pizza business. My dad was interested in a start-up business an acquaintance named Jim Larkin had started in Corning, Iowa. The idea was to get in on a small take-out only pizza business that was doing well and starting to sell franchises.

One of my dad's characteristics was a relentless pursuit of any concept that he found intriguing. Like many personality traits, that was both a strength and a weakness.

After he promoted the concept for a year, I finally appeased him just to get him off my back. We set up a Saturday meeting to check it out. Together we drove one hour east to Corning, Iowa, the closest location and home of the first Breadeaux Pizza.

The business was located in a tiny space next to a Casey's gas station. After sampling the pizza, I had to admit it tasted amazing. I found myself intrigued. When the franchisor told me I could open a store for under $30,000, I was even more intrigued. The concept was to sell pizzas at a low cost—buy one, get one free. Because it was takeout only, there was no need for a big location or large staff. Another part of the idea was to only put the stores in small towns with low rent costs and few competitors. The pizza was good, and you could get two small single-ingredient pizzas for $5.99. It checked all the boxes for a winning idea.

The week following our tour, I called Mr. Larkin and told him I wanted to be his fourth franchise, but I wanted to put it in Council Bluffs, not in a small town. He thought because we were from Glenwood, that's where we'd locate it, but I'd recently moved to Council Bluffs, and we could run it easier without driving to Glenwood.

It took me a week or two to convince him, but he agreed. Over the next few months, we worked with Mr. Larkin and a couple of people he'd brought on board to design the store and order the equipment. We also went to Corning to learn how to make pizza! My wife Karen and I learned how to make and throw the dough in the air, fold boxes, make the sauce, operate the equipment, and all other components of running a pizza operation. It felt fun, new, and exciting for us. Quite a detour from the real estate business.

My first store, located on Creek Top Street in Council Bluffs, Iowa, was twenty-two feet by twenty-two feet, and the equipment took up most of the shop. We had a super small lobby, just six feet long and four feet wide. It cost us $28,000 to open the location after all was said and done.

In truth, we had no idea how well it would go over and if it'd be a screaming success or complete failure. The first week, we made dozens of pizzas and took them to businesses, schools, gyms, or anywhere we could think of, giving them away as samples. Thankfully, people enjoyed the pizza. The phone started ringing, and within two weeks, we had to stop giving away free samples and start building the business.

By the end of the first month, we were getting bombarded with orders on Friday and Saturday nights. By the end of three months, we were slammed all day and night with orders every day of the week. We'd started with two conveyor ovens and had to expand to three, which took up the little remaining space.

That first summer on the weekends, the wait to get a pizza was well over an hour. We had to not only train our staff to handle the high volume, but we also had to train our loyal customers. People would call in on Thursday, asking to reserve two pizzas for 7:00 p.m. on Friday night. Hell, you would have thought we were some kind of fine dining establishment.

I'll never forget one lady driving in twenty miles from Crescent, Iowa, to get two pizzas. I talked to her for a moment while she waited in the lobby.

"I don't know how you can make any money selling two small pizzas for $5.99," she said.

"We lose money on every pizza," I said, "but we make it up with volume."

She gave me a serious look for a moment. Then her face lit up. "Oh! That makes sense."

She didn't get the joke.

We were up to our elbows in flour and sauce seven days a week. We were shocked, overwhelmed, and thrilled all at the same time.

The first year, we netted a profit of over $125,000. It couldn't have turned out better. So, if one franchise is good, two is better, right? And if two work, then why not five or ten? I could see the money pouring into our bank account. I was high from success and wanted to keep pushing for more. After all, in business there's a saying, "If you're not growing, you're dying."

You can see how at this point I might have thought my original dream needed modification. To hell with real estate! I want to make more of that kind of dough! (Pun intended). So Karen and I opened a second store on the east end of Council Bluffs on Woodbury Avenue. This store was double the size of our first one and designed to handle big volume. It cost us about $70,000 to open, and while it didn't profit as much as the first store, it still felt like we were printing money.

We worked hard and did every job there was to do, from making pizza to cleaning bathrooms to chopping onions. I was thirty years old at the time and lacked the GPS programming to slow down and double-check my route. All I could think about was expand, expand, expand. Because I was so involved in the day-to-day grind, I never took the time to step back and evaluate the business from a distance.

One day a curveball came flying into town. The ace pitcher who threw it was named Pizza Hut. They offered both takeout and delivery. Along with a big marketing budget, Pizza Hut had an instant edge on us with their delivery option. I remember approaching the owners of Breadeaux Pizza with my concerns, asking if we could offer delivery, but they were against it. When you're the franchisee, the franchisor makes all the rules, and if they say no, then it's no. If you ignore them, they can close your store.

In 1988, three years into the pizza business, we were struggling but remained optimistic. We knew some of our stores were losing money, but we were obligated to leases and loans and felt that if we could get their sales volumes up, we could turn them around.

We increased advertising for those stores and tried to identify any problems with staff, service, quality, etc. Much of our competition was moving to delivery, and again, our franchisor wouldn't allow us to deliver when I asked a second time.

With our competitive edge gone, we were in deep trouble.

I'd think to myself that if I could find another location, that'd be a home-run store like our first store. It would bail us out. But inside, I knew more growth and more debt weren't the answer. I'd already tried that way too many times, and it only made things worse.

Looking back later, it's easy to see what happened. We grew too fast and took on too much debt and too much work. A note to young entrepreneurs: Growth eats cash and stresses every part of your organization. Be careful. If only 1985 Jerry knew that.

By the summer of 1990, we'd reached the pinnacle—of something terrible.

We were managing thirteen stores spread from Glenwood, Iowa, to Columbus, Nebraska. Several were in Omaha and surrounding small towns. Financial and work life pressure reached its peak. One summer night I couldn't sleep, so I went out on our deck. I looked at the night sky and asked myself a hard question: "What the hell are you doing?"

As a family, we were all working our asses off seven days a week, and a twelve-hour day felt light. In the mornings, we were moving products from store to store, trying to hire employees, fix equipment, deal with staff issues, and pay bills. Our stores were open from noon to ten, and it was a consistent issue that someone would not show up, or we'd have to rush to a store to deal with a problem.

That evening, I took honest stock of everything going on, and I came to an earth-shaking summary of affairs. We were more than

$650,000 in debt, plus another $150,000 in accounts payable with vendors hounding us about past-due bills. Seven of our thirteen stores were losing money. When I did the analysis, the other six didn't make up the difference. We had no savings left, and our house was mortgaged to its maximum. Reality had hit home. Everything was wrong with this picture. I knew it was over.

Nothing could save us now.

I picked up the phone at 3:00 a.m. and called my accountant and my attorney. I left them both voicemails saying I needed to meet first thing in the morning. I met with each and laid it all out. I think it was the first time in over a year that I'd been honest with them and, sadly, myself. I'd been avoiding the facts and sugarcoating everything with unrealistic optimism.

At the end of both meetings, their advice was the same. File for bankruptcy.

That was a gut punch.

From my days in real estate, I knew that would ruin our credit for years to come, and my pride couldn't handle the embarrassment of bankruptcy. Three years earlier, I'd been the chairman of the Council Bluffs Chamber of Commerce. I'd been featured in numerous news articles and seen as an entrepreneurial mover and a shaker in our community of 56,000. No way could I file for bankruptcy!

I had to find an alternative, but the more important concern went back to the relationship aspect I discussed earlier. I knew some of my creditors were friends and mentors. How could I ask my insurance agent and friend Dick Davis to lose any of the money I owed him? How could I hang my banker and friend Skip Starr out to dry? I couldn't do that to them. They'd trusted and believed in me.

So I concocted a plan. I'd try to get the franchisor Jim Larkin to buy me out. His competitive drive was bigger than an extra-large supreme pizza. He constantly challenged me to expand more. I felt like he believed he would make the stores succeed better than I could.

A few days later, we met at the corporate offices in St. Joseph, Missouri, where they'd moved to from Corning a year or two earlier. The meeting took place in a conference room with Jim Larkin and two executives. After some small talk, they gave me an update on what was going on within the franchise system. They told me about new franchises they'd sold, new advertising they were working on, new products they were testing, and so on. The mood was positive. It felt like they wanted me to join in the excitement, but I was there for different reasons. After all the buildup and bright future outlook stuff was over, they started asking me questions.

"Jerry, how are things going for you and your stores?"

"You know, Jim, some stores are good, some are breaking even, and others are losing."

"Well, that's how it goes sometimes. You'll get the losers back on par soon enough."

"Well, the truth is cash flow is tight, and Karen and I are working outrageous hours."

"We all go through those times, especially during expansion. Speaking of expansion, when are you planning on expanding in Omaha? Adding some more stores in Omaha will offset the poor performers in those smaller markets. You'll be able to do more metro-wide marketing and get better managerial help to cut down on your in-store hours."

One executive chimed in, "That's a good point, Jim. Omaha is hot, and it's only going to keep growing."

They were putting on a big pitch for me to buy more franchises.

"I can't see expansion happening for at least another three years minimum with where we're at now. It can only happen if we get our existing stores turned around."

"Jerry, the time is now. The opportunity will not exist in three years. It probably won't exist in one year. You need to see the big picture. In this business, you have to strike while the oven is hot. If you're not willing to take the baton, we'll have to find someone who is ready and give them your Omaha franchise rights."

That was the turn in the conversation I was waiting for.

"I hate to say this, but the reality is my ability to borrow money for more stores is maxed out. If you want me to open new stores in Omaha, I'll have to close some of my other stores to free up capital."

It was not the response they were hoping for, but I was making progress on my plan. The frustration showed on their faces.

"Jerry, this meeting is about Breadeaux Pizza franchise growth. You've always been one of our top franchisees. We didn't expect to hear this from you today."

"I didn't expect things to go this way either. If you're not happy with my growth and performance, maybe you should just buy me out."

That was it. I'd made my play. I wasn't sure how they would take it, but I'd found the perfect place to take my shot. After some silent contemplation, Jim spoke. "Okay. I'm open to that. Give me a number."

I'd already done an analysis before asking for the meeting and determined my bottom line was to cover my bank debt and accounts payable.

"$800,000."

Jim scratched something on his notepad. He didn't look at me or the other two executives. About a minute later, which felt like an hour, he looked up from his pad.

"Give me a week to look at some things, but I'm leaning toward yes."

That was the end of the meeting. I left their offices and made the one-and-a-half-hour drive back to Council Bluffs, feeling optimistic that bankruptcy could be avoided. A few days later, they called me and said they would buy ten of my thirteen stores for $650,000.

Unknown to me, they'd met my banker and had worked out a deal to acquire my debt for the ten stores. It wasn't the number I wanted, but I accepted the deal. I had just reduced my hurdle from $800,000 to $150,000. We closed the transaction a couple of weeks later.

The end was bittersweet, but I knew it was the right move.

THE 5 KEYS TO DETERMINATION

The 5 Keys to Determination are inspired by how my dad, Lloyd Banks, lived his life.

1. **Work Ethic:** Dad's journey began in Creston, Iowa, where, by the age of twelve, he was already balancing multiple jobs—from sorting and stacking bakery items to delivering newspapers and cleaning chicken cage pans. His determination to succeed was clear in his work ethic and willingness to take on any job (no matter how challenging or unappealing) to achieve his goals.

2. **Continuous Development:** Despite his busy work schedule, Dad found time to pursue his passion for exhibition roller skating. He performed all across Southwest Iowa. His dedication to continuous skill development, even outside his immediate professional endeavors, showcases the importance of balancing work with personal growth and interests.

3. **Whatever-It-Takes Attitude:** Dad's career at the CB&Q Railroad, which later became the Burlington Northern Railroad, exemplified his "whatever it takes" attitude. Starting from humble beginnings, carrying furnace ashes and picking up papers, my dad ascended to the role of a conductor. His unwavering work fueled this climb ethic and determination to progress, regardless of the task at hand.

4. **Develop a Vision:** Dad's transition to real estate development, where he built around 2,000 homes in Southwest Iowa, highlighted his visionary approach. He was not just building houses; he was creating communities and homes for hundreds of families, driven by a commitment to quality, honesty, and innovation in energy efficiency. Dad's ability to see and seize opportunities for growth and development underlines a key aspect of determination: vision.

5. **Cultivate an Attitude of Love:** Perhaps the most profound lesson from Lloyd's life is the role of attitude and love. On his 100th birthday, he emphasized the importance of maintaining a positive attitude, loving others, and letting love guide one's actions. His belief that attitude impacts one's health and success serves as a reminder that determination is not just about what we do, but also about how we approach life and interact with others.

STAY DETERMINED TO KEEP GOING

After Jim agreed to buy my other stores, I was left dealing with two stores that were losing money. I had an obligation of over $150,000 in accounts payable. I closed the remaining two stores and sold off the equipment for pennies on the dollar to a man named Sam who was opening a new pizza place in Council Bluffs named Lansky's.

I went to my banker and friend Skip Starr to try to get my remaining debts settled for a lower amount. Skip and I had enjoyed an excellent relationship and friendship up to this point. I'd moved all my Century 21 banking to him a few years earlier when my previous bank, First National Bank of Council Bluffs, was sold, and my friend Stan Duysen had retired.

I was on Skip's bank advisory board and often gave him advice on real estate loans the bank was making. During this time, Skip went through a divorce and asked me to sell his home with zero commission.

I remember saying, "Wait a minute, Skip. I do business with you and pay you interest. Now you want to do business with me but don't want to pay our fees? That doesn't seem quite fair."

He told me he understood my position, but he needed it as a personal favor and would make it up to me in the future. So I put my trust in Skip and in our relationship and agreed to take his listing at no fee.

The time for my favor came. When I told Skip where I was with my pizza business and that I needed a loan to pay off my past-due debts, he told me he believed in me, but after looking at my financial statement said that if he offered me a loan, his bank auditors would challenge it. He suspected they would criticize the bank and make them put up loss reserves to match the loan amount. He explained everything and included all the technical reasons he couldn't make me the loan to make sure I understood.

"Okay, Skip. I understand why you shouldn't make me the loan." I paused and looked him in the eye. "But will you make me the loan?"

He locked his eyes on mine for a moment. Then he chuckled and said, "Yes."

That was the first and only time I've ever given a banker a hug to seal a transaction. I didn't bring it up, but I'm sure he remembered when I helped him out during his divorce, and he put our relationship first, as I did for him just a few years earlier.

Over the next few weeks, I met face to face with every one of my creditors and gave them three choices. I told them option one was me paying twenty cents on the dollar of what I owed, and I'd do so within thirty days. Option two was I'd pay dollar for dollar what I owed if they stopped all interest and penalties. They'd need to agree to payments over several years, and I couldn't guarantee a time frame. Option three was I'd file bankruptcy, and they would get one to five cents on the dollar.

All my vendors and creditors appreciated the honest face-to-face meetings. I was fortunate that most of the creditors took the twenty cents on the dollar. A couple took the dollar-for-dollar option, agreeing to get paid whenever I was able. After Skip loaned me the money, I paid the ones I had agreed to pay twenty cents on the dollar.

I avoided bankruptcy. Again.

Here is where determination came into play. My ego and self-confidence were destroyed. I felt like the entire community looked at me as a loser. My relationship with Karen was on the rocks. I felt everything that went wrong was my fault. I started slipping into what I called a "funk." I think a therapist would've more correctly called it depression. I didn't want to be seen in public. I didn't want to go to my kids' school events. I'd drive them and drop them off but not go in. I withdrew into almost total isolation.

Adding to this dark place was not earning any income. I remember lying awake at night wondering how I would keep the utilities to our home from being shut off later in the week. What could I do to find a few hundred dollars to buy groceries and pay the past-due bills?

Determination got me to the other side, but it was still a detour from my previous dream—one that had become a nightmare.

After a couple of weeks, I started to rebound. I determined this event would not measure me. Since I'd not be measuring myself, I sure as hell didn't want others to measure me and think I was done. I was in my late thirties and came to the correct determination that I had plenty of runway in front of me. I embraced the chance to make amends and prove to the world that one setback did not define me.

My young kids didn't know how big an inspiration they were in my emotional recovery. When I looked into their eyes, I knew I had to pick myself up and get back in the game. I wanted to not just provide for them, but I needed to be a positive role model.

I made a solemn promise to myself. I determined this event of going broke in the pizza business would not define me. During this time, I adopted the mantra that "life is a marathon, not a sprint," which became part of my daily GPS programming routine. I decided I wouldn't measure myself in terms of success or failure at this stage of my life. I knew others would measure and judge me whenever or however they wished. But for me, I would concentrate on running the marathon, one step at a time, and not worry so much about my current position in the race.

If I was ever going to measure myself on those terms, it would be—to borrow a sport's saying—when it's time to hang up my cleats. Measuring oneself in terms of failure or success is a dangerous game to play. If you measure yourself when you're in a rut, all you see is negativity. Conversely, if you measure yourself when you're on top and doing great, you risk becoming too full of yourself, which is equally dangerous. Part of determining your GPS input is not worrying about how society or your peers measure you. Life and business are an endurance race. Program determination to run the marathon to the best of your ability, and do your best to keep moving forward. As long as you keep pushing, you will make progress, and before you know it, you'll be in a better place and be a better person for it.

You might even pick up a new skill along the way—like tossing pizza dough!

YOUR GPS INPUT CHECKLIST

- Bad decisions are learning opportunities when you reflect on them with honesty.
- When challenges arise, don't abandon the goal—get creative.
- Setbacks don't define you—it's how you respond that defines you.
- Life is a marathon, not a sprint. Run your race accordingly.
- Measuring yourself in terms of failure or success is a dangerous game.

CHAPTER 7

RESILIENCY YIELDS THE BIGGEST RETURNS

*"When we long for a life without difficulties,
remind us that oaks grow strong in contrary winds
and diamonds are made under pressure."*

—Peter Marshall

WALK AWAY EVEN WHEN IT HURTS

When you lose control of life's steering wheel, you must stay resilient and trust you'll come out whole on the other side. Sometimes you have to do things you don't want to do to survive, but you must never sacrifice your ethics or values for a paycheck. Staying resilient, even when you don't know if the payoff will come, is often the hardest thing to do, especially when you're in a place that feels like you keep losing. Abandoning your ethics and values also pays—in negative returns. I've always held the belief that good things happen to good people and that the opposite side of that equation also holds true.

I had firsthand experience with this in 1985 when I took a significant detour from my dream venturing into the pizza business. I survived, but things got worse before they got better. Whatever feelings of relief I had from avoiding bankruptcy a second time didn't last long since, with no work and still in debt, my marriage suffered, and the bills kept piling in. My confidence was shot. I'd climbed the mountaintop, only to have it crumble beneath my feet. I felt defeated, but quitting wasn't an option because I wasn't just taking care of me. I had a wife and two daughters who depended on me. Whatever emotions I felt, I had to shove them down into the darkness of my gut and keep going.

Survival mode kicked in, and every day became a struggle.

During that depressing season of my life, I sulked around a grocery store one day trying my best to buy the family food staples on our meager budget when I ran into a business acquaintance, a man I knew from my time in the real estate world. He remembered my successful track record in real estate and asked what I was doing now. I felt embarrassed to tell the truth, but I did, admitting I was looking for new work. To my surprise, he told me he might have something and to come see him the following Monday. I didn't even bother to ask what it was. I just felt grateful for a new opportunity.

When we met at his office, he told me about a newly formed partnership that he and a business associate had started. They were purchasing properties that had been foreclosed on by HUD and were operated by HUD, the US Government Department of Housing and Urban Development. The properties were apartment complexes—100 percent subsidized Section 8 properties.

The company had already purchased a few properties and was raising investor funds to buy more. During our meeting, my friend said they needed someone to do due diligence on potential target properties and help them assess what the returns would be. For the properties they'd already acquired, he wanted me to assist with finding and overseeing management. Because I was desperate for any form of income and the real estate opportunity directly aligned with my CCIM training, I accepted the job on the spot.

Most of the properties were in Houston, Dallas, Tulsa, and Wichita Falls. I soon found out that the majority of the buildings were in tough locations and in horrible condition. Because the properties had been so poorly managed and the tenant profiles were unreliable, it made it nearly impossible to manage rent collection.

Property management people often grade the profiles of properties as Class A on the high end, all the way down to Class D on the lowest end. These would have rated as Class F. Locally, people knew them as "the projects" with all the bad connotations that comes with that name. My job was to do research, analyze, and function as the asset manager. Most of the residents in surrounding neighborhoods hated our complexes. I even got called into city council meetings to defend what we were doing.

One of the most difficult things I had to do was evict people for breaking regulations or for nonpayment. Sometimes it broke my heart because they were trying and just couldn't find the money. Other times I got angry seeing those who could pay choose to be belligerent and threatening instead of doing the right thing. I even remember washing blood off a sidewalk one afternoon from a knifing at one of our locations in Houston. I shudder thinking back to having gang members we were trying to evict from a property threaten my life.

It was sad and frustrating, and I hated it. But I needed the work. I was still paying off creditors from the pizza business. The job was depressing, but I had health insurance for my family and enough money to buy groceries. I was making $50,000 a year with a promise that maybe someday I would get a bonus.

The partnership I worked for obtained all their equity capital from investors. One of those investors they called on to invest was a man named Allan Lozier. The Lozier Corporation is headquartered in Omaha, Nebraska, with factories across the United States. Today the corporation remains the leading manufacturer of shelving used by retailers in stores and warehouses.

Mr. Lozier and one of the principals from my company met to discuss some financial projections related to the properties. Because of that meeting, they set up a subsequent meeting between me and Sheri Andrews to review the financial history, assumptions, and projections for returns on the properties they were considering investing in.

Sheri was the chief financial officer of Lozier Enterprises, which functioned as the holding company for all the Lozier family operations and investments, including the Lozier Corporation. Sheri and I met in Houston so she could tour some of our properties firsthand. Our personalities clicked from the start, but I felt like I was walking a tightrope between being honest with Sheri and doing my best to represent my employer. One of Sheri's many attributes is that not only is she incredibly intelligent, but she can read people. I think she sensed my internal struggle that day.

I knew the profile of these properties wasn't good, and the one they had set up for her to tour was the best of the bunch. We toured units and went over the financials. Sheri asked excellent questions and soon realized the ultra-tough tenant profile and related risk these properties represented. Ultimately, Sheri advised Mr. Lozier not to invest in the venture. I was never given her reasoning, but I suspected it was the risk profile.

Several months after my meeting with Sheri, in early 1992, I discovered some information about the company that made me very uneasy—actually, beyond uneasy! They asked me to put together spreadsheets on properties they owned with unrealistic speculations for potential outcomes that would improve the property value enormously on paper. The numbers projected on the spreadsheets were speculative beyond reasonable expectations. I felt there was no way the properties could ever meet the outcomes shown. I was honest with my bosses that this was unrealistic and a waste of time. The response I got was I shouldn't worry about it because they just wanted to see possibilities.

My suspicions were confirmed shortly thereafter when I learned they were using unreasonably speculative projections to raise money from investors and touting them as actual performance versus speculative. These were the very projections they had asked me to compile for them earlier.

The night after learning the partnership was using false projections I'd compiled, I thought long and hard about what I should do. I was faced with a difficult decision. In reality, I needed the job. I was still in deep debt from my pizza venture, and I had a family to support. But I also knew their activity was at a minimum unethical—and likely illegal.

If I was scapegoated as the one who authored the spreadsheets, then I might get pulled into the public relation and legal nightmares. I knew my reputation would be ruined when this house of cards fell apart. I have a saying I use as a guiding light when faced with situations like this: "It's not a matter of *who* is right; it's a matter of *what* is right."

As I considered my options during that difficult evening, I felt I had no choice but to disassociate from the partnership as fast as possible, regardless of the financial ramifications. I knew in time I could fix my financial issues, but fixing a horrible reputation is a far more difficult proposition. And more important, to live with myself, I had to live true to my core values. I couldn't participate in unethical activity.

I had no job prospects, no savings, and I was deeply in debt. But I did the right thing. I submitted my resignation. That decision was the first step toward a life-changing course reroute that opened new doors to my dreams. In fact, making that difficult but right decision changed my life.

THE 6 KEYS TO LIVING WITH RESILIENCY

1. **Accept Responsibility:** Acknowledge you're in charge of your own future and destiny. Life may throw unexpected challenges your way, but it's your responsibility to navigate through them and stay true to your values, even in tough times.
2. **Embrace Change:** Understand that change is inevitable, and sometimes you may need to walk away from situations, even when it hurts. Resilience involves adapting to change and finding alternative paths to achieve your dreams.
3. **Adopt a Survival Mindset:** In the face of adversity, such as financial struggles or personal setbacks, it's crucial to enter survival mode. This means pushing through emotions and focusing on the necessities to keep moving forward.
4. **Maintain Ethical Integrity:** Stay true to your moral compass, even when faced with unethical situations. The decision to disassociate from unethical practices, despite financial or personal risks, is foundational to living with resiliency.
5. **Stay Open to Opportunity:** New opportunities, even when they come from unexpected sources, can make all the difference. Resilience involves being adaptable and ready to seize chances that can lead to positive changes in your life.
6. **Persist Through Uncertainty:** The journey to success is often filled with uncertainties. Resilient individuals continue to push forward, even when the outcome is unclear, trusting that their efforts will eventually pay off.

RESILIENCY IS A SUPERPOWER

A few weeks after submitting my resignation, I contacted Sheri Andrews to reintroduce myself and tell her I had left the employment of that company.

I remember her comment. "Good decision, Jerry."

I told her I was looking to put together capital investors to purchase market rate apartment complexes in Texas. Then I asked if she thought Mr. Lozier would have any interest in investing with me? She asked me to come see her later in the week.

As I mentioned earlier, the Lozier Corporation was and remains the leading manufacturer of shelving retailers in stores and warehouses. If you walk into just about any Target, Walgreens, or other major retailer, you'll find that Lozier manufactured all or most of the shelves. Lozier Enterprises is the unofficial name for a collection of enterprises and investments owned by Allan Lozier and his family prior to Allan's passing in 2021. This includes the manufacturing enterprise, banking enterprises, a steel foundry company, stocks, bonds, the Lozier Foundation, and of course, real estate.

I didn't know what to expect during my upcoming meeting with Sheri, but the fact that I was meeting with a company of this stature gave me hope. As an unemployed husband and father, anything, even a short-term one-off deal, would help.

I arrived at the Lozier building ready to give my best pitch to Sheri. I'd spent days preparing, knowing she was a pro and every little detail supporting my case would be valuable. As soon as I arrived, Lisa Hansen, Sheri's administrative assistant, promptly took me to Sheri's desk.

"Jerry, good to see you again."

"Great to see you, Sheri. Thank you for taking this meeting."

I thought we'd chitchat for a bit, then I'd work my way into the presentation. I was wrong. As soon as I sat down, Sheri took control.

"Look Jerry, I appreciate you coming in, but Mr. Lozier doesn't have an interest in partnerships."

And just like that, even before I could make a case, the door slammed in my face. The days of preparation were all for naught. I was stunned and struggled to find a response.

"Oh. Okay," I said, shuffling my files in my hand. "I guess you don't want to see these."

"I have a proposition for you. We're potentially looking to hire someone to start a real estate investment portfolio for the Lozier family. Would you have any interest in applying for the position?"

Again, I was stunned.

I went from optimistic, to kicked into a ditch, to now being offered the opportunity to work for one of the biggest and most successful businesses in the country. Talk about a roller coaster of emotions. I did my best not to show my desperate gratitude for the opportunity.

"Well, Sheri, I didn't expect this, but yes, I suppose I would like to know more about the opportunity."

"You'd like to apply for the position?"

"Yes, I would."

That moment led to a series of meetings that lasted for over three months.

Sheri would meet with me most Tuesdays and Thursdays. On Tuesday she'd give me a yellow sheet of paper with a series of hand-written questions from Mr. Lozier about my theories on investment real estate, portfolio building, financing, and portfolio management. I'd take the questions home and type up a white paper response. Then I'd return on Thursday to review my ideas with Sheri. The following week, we'd meet on Tuesday to review Mr. Lozier's responses, along with a new set of questions.

During this three-month "job interview," we never once talked about the job description, salary, or company benefits. It was a nose-to-the-grindstone test of my thinking process and my theories in real estate. Later came questions that tested the application of my ideas and suggestions.

Many times during the process I just wanted to say, "Enough! Do I have the job or not?" It felt like I was writing a handbook on how to buy and hold investment real estate. If I wasn't hired, I'd have given away a valuable manual of information. But I needed the job, and all my instincts told me I could trust Sheri, so I stayed determined to see the process through. I did wonder what might happen if, after all this work, they passed on me. That was a real risk that crossed my mind more than once, but I trusted I was demonstrating my competence, so sticking it out should pay off. All the while at home we were surviving on credit cards and the meager earnings from a job Karen had taken.

At the end of three months, Sheri told me it was time for me to meet Allan. She scheduled an appointment for me on Thursday, October 29, 1992, at 10:30 a.m. I hadn't yet met Allan Lozier, so I had no idea what to expect. I did remember my father had built a house in Glenwood for an engineer who'd worked several years with Mr. Lozier at the Lozier Corporation. I knew this engineer well enough, so I called him and asked for his thoughts about what to expect at the meeting with Mr. Lozier. He told me Allan rarely met with people and that the meetings were always short. He guessed it would likely be a five-minute meet and greet. I was relieved to hear that, so that's what I mentally prepared for on the day of my "interview" with Mr. Lozier.

Once I arrived, Allan's office seemed surprisingly economical—not the opulent office of a rich guy I'd imagined. Books lined the back wall, and his ordinary office desk stood next to another four-person table for meetings.

The first thing I noticed about Allan Lozier was his size. At six feet eight inches tall, he was an imposing figure to meet. Since I was already nervous, I consoled myself by remembering my friend said Allan preferred short meetings. It turned out that scouting report was way off. For the next hour and a half, Allan grilled me on every topic imaginable. He had a thick stack of papers in front of him with notes written all over the margins. The stack included my résumé and all the white papers I had written over the prior three months.

First he dug into my Century 21 experience from over a decade ago. Then he asked business and personal questions related to the pizza business failure. They weren't insulting, but he wanted to know my perspective on what happened and what I learned. He also asked about my goals, my parents, and other personal questions. I thought to myself, "What does this have to do with what you'll possibly hire me to do?" I felt like he was stripping me down and exposing all my weaknesses. I did the only thing I could think of: I was as open and honest as possible.

After ninety minutes, he had worked through the stack of documents.

I felt mentally exhausted, wondering what he'd throw at me next.

Allan picked up the pile of papers between us and set them aside. Then he swiveled his chair around to his desk and started to work on something. I sat in silence, waiting for him to say something or turn back around.

He didn't.

After an uncomfortable amount of time passed, I leaned over in my chair and looked toward the door. Thankfully, I made eye contact with his admin, Ginny. She signaled for me to exit. As I rose from my chair, Allan didn't budge or turn to say goodbye to me. Making my way to the door, I looked back at Allan, but he never looked my way.

Finally, I was out and standing in front of Ginny. I'd survived.

"What just happened?" I asked her.

"He's done."

I didn't know what to think. I felt good about my transparent responses, but I couldn't gauge how Allan had received them. Sheri Andrews wasn't around, so I left the building and headed home, feeling bewildered. That day I experienced one of Mr. Lozier's idiosyncrasies. At the conclusion of our meeting, he never said, "We're done," or "Thank you for coming in." He just turned his chair around and started working on something else. Over time, I learned this was his typical behavior. He didn't bother with conventional courtesies.

I'd just made my way home and walked through the door when the phone rang.

"Jerry," Sheri asked, "what happened in your meeting with Allan?"

"I have no idea. You tell me! All I can tell you is he grilled me for an hour and a half."

"Stay by the phone. I'll call you right back."

Thirty minutes later, the phone rang.

"You've got the job. Can you start on Tuesday morning at 8:00 a.m.?"

My head spun.

"Wait a minute, Sheri. We haven't talked about salary or benefits."

"Don't worry about that, Jerry. We'll work it all out next week. See you Tuesday?"

In the past I would've never accepted a job like this, but I was desperate and felt like these were good people. The company had an outstanding reputation, so I trusted my gut and said, "Yes. See you Tuesday."

Tuesday, November 2, 1992, would be the first day of a twenty-three-plus year career working for Allan Lozier. His office building is located in a one-story, 80,000-square-foot structure with only a few private offices. The majority of staff work for the manufacturing enterprise and sit in open landscape pods about eight feet by eight feet, with five-foot-tall fabric-covered, movable partitions. On my first day, Sheri hunted around the treasury department to find an empty pod for me but couldn't find one. She ended up putting me in a temporary location in the shelving installation department.

The offices of Lozier were nice and efficient but anything from fancy. The decor was somewhere between a government office building and Class B office—just slightly better than your local Social Security office. Conference rooms had the only windows, except for a few open areas and Allan's office itself. No other private offices had windows. Within a couple of weeks, I was moved to a pod within the treasury department.

For several years, Dianne—Allan's wife and the chief counsel for the company—worked about four pods down from me. Status and hierarchy in the Lozier company was pretty flat, with Allan at the top of the food chain, which everyone knew. He ignored egos, status, and rank and reserved no parking spots for himself or executives. No one received special privileges. Whenever vendors delivered lunch, everyone stood in line in the order they arrived, including Allan or any other executive. I loved and respected that about the company.

I recall a story that illustrated the company lacked tolerance for big egos within their operations. At one point, they hired a new senior vice president of sales and marketing. On his first day at work, he drove a Mercedes convertible into the parking lot. His clothes, shoes, and entire persona screamed "big ego." I didn't meet the guy for several weeks, but the rumors around the office were this guy wouldn't last. Everyone said his ego would show itself, and he'd be gone soon. They were right. He lasted less than six months.

Over the next two-plus decades, our real estate investment division of Lozier Enterprises, which I was the leader of, completed over $1.5 billion in investment real estate transactions. This included buying and renovating apartment complexes, shopping centers, office buildings, and more. We codeveloped condo projects. We financed subdivision developments. We acquired and leased warehouses. We were active in almost every type of real estate activity in the investment field except for hotels, which we never ventured into. Our properties were located in places such as Phoenix, Salt Lake City, Dallas, Fort Worth, San Antonio, Austin, Philadelphia, Mississippi, Wisconsin, West Virginia, and more. This life-changing opportunity not only made me a lot of money, but I also grew as a person, learned a ton, and progressed in my thinking about investments, philanthropy, life, and more. Enormous gratitude is an understatement for trying to explain the feelings I have for the opportunity Sheri and the entire Lozier family and organization gave me in 1992.

Had it not been for some difficult but ultimately fortuitous decisions, this life-changing opportunity never would have happened. If I'd filed for bankruptcy when the pizza business fell apart, Lozier likely wouldn't have hired me. Had I not decided to quit my employment at the partnership running HUD foreclosed properties, I probably would never have called Sheri Andrews about potential real estate investments. If I'd thrown in the towel during the three-month interview process, I would've never worked for Lozier.

Good decisions, determination, and staying disciplined all came together to bring about this life-changing series of events for me and my family. Did I see it at the time? Of course not. But in hindsight, I know these factors played a huge role in being influenced by my own internal GPS helping me arrive at one of my biggest dream destinations: a leader in commercial real estate investments, financial security, abundance for my family, and ultimately, my own real estate investment company.

YOUR GPS INPUT CHECKLIST

- Embrace change and adapt to new circumstances.
- Keep pushing forward, even when facing personal and professional challenges.
- Seize new opportunities but remain vigilant.
- Uphold your ethical standards, even when it's more lucrative to compromise them.
- Trust your abilities to maintain a positive attitude when your path forward is unclear.

CHAPTER 8

ARRIVING AT YOUR DREAM DESTINATION

"The capacity to learn is a gift; the ability to learn is a skill;
the willingness to learn is a choice."

—Brian Herbert

NEVER STOP LEARNING

As you make your way in life and in your career, often it'll feel like you're driving at night, only able to see twenty feet ahead. Even when your vision is limited, you have to trust that staying the course will get you to your destination. Although you can't see the payoff now, having the discipline to keep learning can be the thing that gets you to your dream destination. This philosophy isn't just about acquiring new knowledge or skills, but about maintaining a sense of curiosity, openness, and adaptability in all aspects of life.

Imagine yourself as a traveler on an endless road, where each step forward brings new experiences, challenges, and opportunities for growth. Just as a traveler relies on a map and compass to guide their way, you, too, can rely on the power of learning to steer your journey toward success and fulfillment. Learning is not confined to the walls of a classroom or the pages of a textbook. It's an ongoing process that happens every day, in every interaction, and in every new experience. Whether it's learning from your mistakes, seeking new perspectives, or simply staying curious about the world around you, the spirit of learning can keep you engaged and motivated.

In 1992, at thirty-seven, I'd arrived at my destination—not my final destination but one I'd been working toward for decades, and one that would give me the life I dreamed of for so long. However, at the time, I didn't know how the Lozier position would help me achieve my ultimate dream. I thought I'd be there for a year or two, get my feet back on the ground, then go out on my own again. With minor exceptions, I'd always owned my business or worked in small businesses. I never envisioned myself working as an employee in a firm of over 1,500 people and answering to a CPA. I remember thinking, "Give me two good years, and I'm out of here!"

From high school through my years at Century 21 and Breadeaux Pizza, I'd convinced myself I didn't need college. I knew enough about real estate, development, business, and construction from real-life experiences. I'd prepared myself by reading, researching, and trying to gain knowledge in every area. Yet despite my arrival, my confidence was nowhere close to what you might think it would've been. I still had a lingering self-image struggle from not attending college for one stinking day. In those early days at Lozier, I remember being in meetings, and everybody would start talking about their universities or the football game that weekend. A common question was, "Where did you go to school?" Whenever I thought the question might be coming my way, I'd excuse myself.

"Pardon me. I have to go to the restroom."

I'd go in, wash my hands, stare in the mirror, and wash my hands again, hoping the conversation had shifted. I didn't want to tell anyone

I never went to college. Many of my colleagues had master's degrees. How could I ever have their respect as an equal if they knew I'd never stepped foot on a college campus? I somehow kept this "secret" for almost a decade—until I was forced to face it one day. I could only use the restroom so many times.

During a casual lunch meeting with Mr. Lozier, the finance controller of the manufacturing enterprise, and the vice president of manufacturing, Mr. Lozier started talking about college and education. Then he said something that caused me to look down at my food and pray the moment would pass. But this time I couldn't excuse myself to the restroom. I was trapped.

"Well, everybody in this room has a master's degree."

Everyone nodded except me. It was time for honesty to triumph over self-image. A decade of dodging this moment had taken its toll on my self-esteem. I couldn't take it anymore.

"Excuse me, Allan, I don't have a master's degree."

"I thought you had a master's in finance."

"Allan, I never went to college a day in my life. You saw my résumé when you hired me."

"Where did I get the idea that you do?"

"I have no clue."

Over the years, I imagined how this moment would play out. Some scenarios were worse than others, but they all ended the same way: humiliation. I didn't think I'd get fired, but I imagined it would be, at the least, extremely awkward and could hurt my reputation within the firm. I braced myself for the worst.

"Well, Jerry, you conduct yourself as though you have a master's degree in finance. The work you do and investments in real estate for me, the detailed memos, and the analysis you do, I would've never guessed you don't have a master's. Maybe that's where I got the idea."

And just like that, a massive self-inflicted weight was lifted off my shoulders. Allan didn't care. Nobody cared. I was the only one who cared. It really was just a missing piece of paper in the grand scheme.

My self-imposed negative image had taken up way too much space in my brain and had damaged my self-image.

This brings me again to measuring yourself against others. As I talked about earlier, don't measure yourself early in the game. Life is a marathon, not a sprint. I measured myself for years against a false perception of how I assumed other people would look at me. I did it out of fear. You can take the word "fear" and turn it into the acronym F.E.A.R. that stands for False Evidence Appearing Real.

Allan's kind words of acknowledgment further fueled my decision to learn, learn, and learn some more. Ironically, I hated math in high school, and the highest level of math I ever achieved was general math. I never took a single course in algebra, geometry, or calculus. Who knew I would someday become known as a numbers guy? When I decided on my dream destination of becoming a leader in commercial investment real estate, I knew I had to learn and develop my math skills related to investment and real estate. I never thought I was "bad" at math or gave myself a handicapping label. The story you tell yourself plays a big factor in who you are and become. Thankfully I hadn't fallen into that trap enough to stop me from sharpening my math skills when the time came, even if it wasn't under the supervision of an accredited instructor.

I discovered early in my Certified Commercial Investment Member (CCIM) classes that the basis of a financial calculator and things like discounting to "net present value" or "amortization" are brought to us by the Ellwood Tables. I have the book of tables in my home library and studied them in my early years before transitioning into commercial investment real estate. The Ellwood Tables, written and published in 1959 by L.W. Pete Ellwood, reinvented the appraisal and financial world. The functions that get calculated for us in either a financial calculator or an Excel spreadsheet result from the computerization of the Ellwood Tables. Because of my desire to learn the Ellwood Tables and by doing calculations by hand without the aid of a financial calculator, I developed an ability to look at a number associated with a mortgage payment and know if something was off. If it felt wrong, then I knew some data had to be incorrect. I'm grateful for this ability, which I attribute to my study of the Ellwood Tables and my dedication to lifelong learning.

Today I can do complex math computations in my head. I'm also an Excel spreadsheet wiz. I never took a class or seminar for Excel. I studied the program on my own and read whatever I could find about the topic. I was never shy about asking coworkers or friends for help when I found them using formulas and spreadsheet tricks I hadn't seen before.

All of this self-learning gave me the ability to negotiate transactions that involved millions of dollars, requiring me to persuade Mr. Lozier and his accountants that my analysis was accurate. In one transaction in 2008, we purchased over $70 million worth of warehouses in Wisconsin, Mississippi, Pennsylvania, and West Virginia containing over 1.6 million square feet of space from General Motors. I negotiated both the purchase of the transaction and the lease back to GM. My analysis had to be approved by our internal accountants, a Big Eight accounting firm, and, of course, Mr. Lozier.

Later I renegotiated a new lease with GM at their Detroit office after their 2010 bankruptcy. Those negotiations were between me and the number two executive in the General Motors's real estate division. We renegotiated all four leases in less than a day. Normally such a negotiation might take days or even weeks to accomplish. In 2011 we sold the warehouses back to GM for a very nice profit.

I'm not looking for a pat on the back with these examples of multimillion-dollar commercial real estate deals I brokered. However, I do want to point out that a "non-math guy" who barely graduated from high school accomplished all this, which isn't to downplay the importance of college. I just want to show you how it's possible to overcome deficits in your development at any stage of life with some determination and discipline. A major factor in my success resulted from my decision to be a lifetime learner. Never stop learning, growing, and refining your skills.

SEEK GREAT MENTORS

In your own life and career, one of the most valuable resources you can have is a great mentor who is more than a guide. They are a source of wisdom, experience, and insight that can help you navigate hurdles on your path. That's who Allan Lozier became for me and much more. The benefits of seeking and learning from mentors are immeasurable. A mentor can provide you with perspective and advice that only comes from years of experience. They can help you avoid common pitfalls and make informed decisions. With their guidance, you can develop skills and strategies that would take much longer to learn on your own. A mentor's support can also boost your confidence and motivate you to push beyond your comfort zone.

Mentors also open doors to opportunities and networks that might otherwise be out of reach. They introduce you to influential people, recommend you for positions, and advocate for your growth. But perhaps the most significant benefit of having a mentor is the personal growth that comes from the relationship. Through their feedback and challenges, mentors help you grow not just professionally but also personally. They help you develop a deeper understanding of yourself, your strengths, and your weaknesses, and guide you toward becoming the best version of yourself.

Seeking great mentors is not just about finding someone to give you advice; it's about finding someone who believes in your potential and is invested in your success. When you find such a person, cherish the relationship, learn as much as you can, and remember to pay it forward by mentoring others in the future. Also, remember two very important words when ending every conversation with your mentor: "Thank you." Typically, that's all they want for their time, expertise, and caring.

I learned a lot about what makes a great mentor during my time at Lozier, where I ended up working for twenty-three years and nine months. So much for two years and I'm out of here! After ten years,

I became a partner in the real estate portfolio. During my tenure, we did over $1.5 billion worth of real estate transactions across the nation. We purchased and developed properties from West Virginia to Arizona and owned and operated warehouses, apartment complexes, office buildings, shopping centers, land developments, condos, and more.

I worked hard during those years and left everything I had on the table. As much success as I experienced, the most uniquely valuable thing I got was working alongside a man whom I consider my greatest mentor next to my father. I used to call Allan Lozier the Howard Hughes of Omaha because they were both reclusive, wealthy, and incredibly gifted people. Looking back on my time with Allan, I believe he was a true genius. The experts say anyone with an IQ over 140 is considered a genius. When I think back on how Allan could take in, analyze, and understand information in seconds, I'm certain he had an IQ well over 140. His ability to pull up information from decades ago on the fly also made me think he had a photographic memory.

I remember one instance when we were looking to acquire a 510,000-square-foot industrial building facility in Cedar City, Utah. Allan was analyzing the potential use and cost of electrical for the facility. He asked me to find out how many kilowatts of power the building had used over the past twelve months. I found the utility bills and discovered the company providing power to the building billed in BTUs not kilowatts. I went to Allan and told him I couldn't provide him with the kilowatts because they used BTUs in their billings.

"Jerry, convert the BTUs to kilowatts."

In my mind I thought, "Google," and turned to leave before Allan stopped me.

"You know how to do that, don't you?"

"No, but I'll figure it out."

"It's simple, Jerry. Take the BTUs and multiply it by .000293."

I'm sure my chin hit the floor. Who knows this stuff off the top of their head? In my lifetime, I know of only one person: Allan Lozier.

As impressive as Allan's computational mind was, I found how he dealt with his employees and the people he valued even more impressive. Allan wanted to know the truth and didn't have patience with people who didn't tell him what he needed to hear. More than once he said, "Jerry, I don't always like what you tell me, but I always know it's the truth, and you're one of the people I can count on to tell me the negatives, to tell me where we're going wrong."

People with power and prestige often protect themselves with "yes people." Allan had very few "yes people" around him. He was diligent about surrounding himself with those who would argue or debate him. Being candid and courageous has tremendous value. When you give candid input, though, you have to be willing to receive the same in return and listen. Listening is an extremely valuable tool if you allow it to be a part of your process. If you think you're always right, or you're smarter than everybody else, you're going to have problems. Nobody has a franchise on the best ideas. Having candid conversations in a safe environment is invaluable in business and life. At Lozier, Sheri would often say, "We don't look at a glass of water and ask if it's half full or half empty because it doesn't matter. It's whatever it is. We look at the glass of water and ask, 'What's the plan to fill it?'" That can-do, collaborative philosophy represented the culture of the Lozier organization. It's also a great way of thinking about how to juggle cynicism and optimism.

Whenever I brought an acquisition, development, or sale opportunity to Allan, he followed the same routine, starting with every reason we shouldn't do the deal. He questioned everything and looked at it from every angle to see why it wouldn't work. Allan made both a science and an art out of cynicism. In my early years, this cynical approach intimidated me, but over time I recognized the value, and I grew to love it.

Another gift Allan unknowingly gave me was the name for the Lozier real estate enterprise. For the first fifteen years, we didn't even have a name. Unofficially, we called what I ran "The Lozier Real Estate

Portfolio," but there wasn't an actual company or entity by that name. I had a business card, but we didn't have a brochure or website. As we added retail properties to our portfolio, we needed to name our real estate enterprise to avoid confusion between the Lozier Corporation that manufactured retail store fixtures and Lozier as a landlord.

Allan told me to give him some name suggestions. I don't recall all the suggestions, but the winner was NewStreet Properties. I'd thrown that into the mix as an homage to my parents. Growing up, Dad built homes along an unnamed street in Glenwood. When he'd refer to a home under construction, he'd call it NewStreet. Later, the City of Glenwood named it Grove Street. But in our family, it was forever NewStreet. To my surprise and delight, out of the bunch of options, Allan chose NewStreet Properties as the official name of the Lozier family real estate enterprise. I'm extremely proud to say the name endures to this day. My title became the portfolio director of NewStreet Properties.

In 2005 we determined it was time to exit the multifamily market with a goal to downsize our apartment holdings because the market appeared overheated. The cap rates were too low relative to the cost of capital, and it didn't make sense to maintain those holdings. Over the next twenty-four months, we went from owning over 4,000 apartment units in Dallas, Fort Worth, Phoenix, Omaha, and Salt Lake to owning just over 500 units.

We got off to a good start by exiting our Phoenix, Fort Worth, and Dallas apartment investments, achieving some crazy good returns. Next, I discussed with Allan the prospects of selling the Salt Lake apartment complexes. I assumed Allan would jump on board with my assessment because things went so well with the other properties. I was wrong. He opposed selling two properties that contained over 600 units. I realized Allan had never visited either property and only knew them via my reports, photos, and descriptions. He rarely saw any of the properties we owned. I was confident we would achieve some great pricing if we were to market them immediately.

Two months later, I convinced him to let me try to sell them off market. That meant we weren't going to list them for sale, but I had permission to tell a couple of key brokers we might be interested if we were offered the right price. Within a short amount of time, we received a fantastic offer from an investment group in California. We had less than $20 million in the two properties combined, and their offer was just shy of $48 million. After I told Allan about the offer, he still wasn't convinced we should sell them, even with a $28 million gain on top of the great returns we had experienced over twelve years. I couldn't believe his stubbornness on the issue.

I went back into negotiations with the buyer, and after several sessions of back-and-forth offers, I got the amount raised to $51 million. I could sense that was their last offer, and if we didn't accept, they would walk. I met again with Allan and reported my negotiation success, convinced he'd be happy with my efforts.

He wasn't. He said we would keep it.

I couldn't figure him out. Why was he so adamant about keeping these properties? I slept on his decision overnight, and the more I thought about it, the more convinced I was that we were making a huge mistake. I was determined I had to convince him to change his mind. There was just one minor obstacle in my path. Once Allan made a decision, turning the decision around was like turning around a ship in a frozen river.

I came to Allan the next morning with more information on the marketplace and economy. I unveiled what I believed to be overwhelming data that proved we were receiving an incredible price. I outlined how we wouldn't pay this price for those properties if they were for sale today. It didn't work. He remained against the sale.

As I left his office, I couldn't let it go. He hired me for this very thing. If he'd given me good reasons, I could accept it. But he hadn't. I wasn't going to be a "yes man." I turned around and marched back into his office. I could tell by the look on his face that I was overstaying my welcome. I sat down, looked him square in the eye, and did my honesty thing.

"Allan, I'm convinced you're wrong about not approving this sale. I can also tell you I'm more than willing to be wrong. But, if I'm the one who's wrong, let me be wrong that we sold it when we should have kept it. I don't want to be wrong that we kept it when we should have sold it."

"Finally, you've said something intelligent. Sell it."

Mr. Lozier was always good at throwing jabs at me. He did it often, and he was pretty good at it. Here's the bottom line to this story: If I had not stayed determined through our twenty-four-month process of selling several thousand apartment units in several markets, we would have looked like fools a year later. The profits would have been losses. We went from over 4,000 apartment units to 500 units from the beginning of 2005 to the end of 2007. My staff and I stayed the course with dogged determination to market these properties, negotiate contracts, and close transactions. I spent a ridiculous amount of time on airplanes and in hotels during these twenty-four months traveling from market to market. Without team unity and determination, we would not have realized the gains we made.

And as for Allan? What was his role in this? He pushed me to do my best work and go all in on my assessments. He wouldn't accept me coming to him and saying, "I think this is what we should do." He wanted me to stretch myself to where I was willing to put myself, not just my analysis, on the line. Only when I turned around and came back to his office to take full ownership did he finally approve of the deal. That's what great mentors do. They find ways to get the most out of you.

ADVICE ON SPEAKING YOUR TRUTH

Sometimes I've been a bit too much of a smart-ass or too cocky. Other times something hits me wrong, and I react with a cutting comment. I'm a big proponent of the adage, "Speak your truth and let the chips fall where they may." I think this adage is a good one to employ but never out of anger or with a smart-ass tone. An episode between me and Mr. Lozier serves as a good example of where I spoke my truth but could've handled it far better.

One day Allan popped into my office and handed me information about a real estate transaction, including details about a shopping center that had recently sold in Omaha. We were not involved in that transaction. However, several months earlier we'd acquired an 80 percent ownership interest in ten Omaha shopping centers that were very similar in age, size, location, and tenant profile. At that point, Allan asked me for a point-by-point analysis comparing what we had purchased earlier with this other similar transaction we hadn't purchased.

"Are you in a hurry? I'm very busy this week."

"No hurry—tomorrow morning is fine."

Tomorrow morning? That was Allan.

That evening, working from home, I put together an Excel spreadsheet and laid out ten points for comparison. In column A, I listed the various components for comparison. In column B, I input all the details of the property he wanted me to compare our properties to. In column C, I listed the average of our ten centers on the various points. Columns D through N, I input the information for each individual center. Going down the rows of column A, I listed the various points I was comparing, such as the price per square foot, the occupancy rate at closing, the average rent, the percentage of national tenants in our centers versus the property he wanted it compared to, the age of the properties, and so on. I listed everything I could think of that would give us a good look at how our recent acquisition of the ten centers compared to the other transaction. It took me five hours to put the document together, but it was good, and I hoped Allan would appreciate my efforts.

The next morning, I came to the office early and formatted my Excel spreadsheet for printing. I reviewed all the information again, also going over it with one of my staff members to see if they could think of anything I had missed and if I had done a fair comparison.

When I felt comfortable and ready, I headed to Allan's office. I had a full day ahead of me, and I didn't need this interruption, so I was not in a great mood. Further, we already owned and had closed on our ten centers. If the other deal was a better deal, so what? But the boss wanted to see the information, so I did what he asked.

I brought in two copies of my findings: one for Allan and one for myself. What I had forgotten and only thought about a few days later is that Allan was a speed reader. When I started to discuss the basis of my research, he had already read the document, focused on the most important elements, and had reached his conclusions.

The joys of working with a genius.

"If you'll look here at point one, you'll see the comparison property sold for $95 a square foot, and we paid on average $91 a square foot," I said, waiting for a positive confirmation that we did well.

It didn't come.

"Jerry, do you see a chiropractor often?"

"No. Why?"

"Never mind. Go on."

I returned to my analysis.

"Now if you look here at point two, you'll see the comparison property was 88 percent occupied upon sale, and what we purchased was 93 percent occupied as of closing."

I paused to see if he had a comment or question.

"Jerry, do you have a relative who's a chiropractor?"

"No, Allan, I don't. Why?"

"Never Mind. Go on."

"Okay. You'll see point three shows the comparison property sold at an 8 percent cap rate, and our transaction had an average cap rate across all ten properties of 8.25 percent, so on a cap rate basis, we made a better investment."

"Jerry, do you have close buddies or friends who are chiropractors?"

My patience hit a wall.

"Allan, what are all these questions about chiropractors? I'm trying to go over the information you requested, and you keep asking me about me seeing chiropractors."

"Well, Jerry. You seem to spend so much time patting yourself on the back. I figure you must see a chiropractor on a regular basis."

That hit me wrong.

I'd worked overtime to put this report together at his request, and now he was jabbing me and saying I was bragging. I looked him in the eye and quipped, "Allan, if I could get my head that far up my ass, I might see your point of view."

He arched his back and rolled his chair backward. The smile left his face. I knew I had overstepped my boundary.

"I think I should excuse myself now," I said.

"I think that's a good idea."

I left the papers on his desk and went back to my office. Soon after, I walked around the building to find Sheri Andrews. Other than Dianne Lozier, no one knew Allan better than Sheri. I told her what happened and asked her if I should apologize. After she stopped laughing, she said, "You absolutely should not apologize. First, he'll see it as a sign of weakness. Second, he deserved it. Just lie low and avoid him for a day or two."

That gave me some relief.

The next day, I was walking down the hall and ran into Greg Maring, the VP of sales and marketing. Greg and I were friendly, and when he saw me, he started laughing. "Hey Jerry, glad to see you're still with the company."

The word was out.

"Oh shit. You talked to Sheri?"

"No, I had a meeting this morning with some of the top VPs, along with Allan. He told us that yesterday Jerry Banks told him he had his head up his ass."

"Oh my god." I was shell-shocked.

Greg slapped me on the shoulder. "Don't worry, Jerry. Allan got a kick out of it."

Whew! I dodged a potential land mine. In hindsight, I mishandled that moment with Allan. He was owed more respect than I delivered.

I could have rebuffed his chiropractor comments with something far less crude. I'm not sorry for standing up to him. He deserved it, but I regret being a smart-ass when that wasn't necessary or kind. I didn't take the high road, something I always recommend others do.

Granted, Allan was a notorious jabber. I knew that, and I also knew he never did it to belittle somebody. That day I got so caught up in myself I forgot the relationship side of things and took his jab too personally. But I think it's important that no matter who the audience is, you're comfortable and confident enough to speak your truth and let the chips fall where they may. When you feel the need to say something, ask yourself first, is it true? Second, is it necessary? Third, is it kind? If you get a "no" to any one of those three questions, then don't say it.

Because of the outcome, it's now a funny story, but that's only because of Allan's forgiving reaction. Allan had a good, but very dry, sense of humor. It also illustrates his willingness to take criticism or be told he's wrong and not let his ego take over. Many extremely wealthy types aren't as patient or as forgiving as Allan was in that regard.

Thank you, Allan, for your belief in me, your mentoring, your patience, and your wisdom.

YOUR GPS INPUT CHECKLIST

- Lifelong learning is essential for growth and success.
- Don't let false perceptions manifest into self-doubt.
- Great mentors provide invaluable guidance, wisdom, and opportunities.
- Committing to honesty and transparency at all times builds trust and respect in relationships.
- Speaking your truth is important, but it should be done with consideration, necessity, and kindness.

CHAPTER 9

FORGIVENESS IS A GIFT YOU GIVE YOURSELF

"That which does not kill us makes us stronger."

—Friedrich Nietzsche

TURN TRAGEDY INTO HOPE

When terrible things happen in life, they'll either destroy you or make you stronger. You can lie down and give up, or you can stay determined to be resilient and find a way to get through it. You should also learn from your mistakes and grow, but you can't let them define you. I recommend finding a spark in the darkness and turning it into a blazing inferno.

Two years into my dream job at Lozier, life threw me another devastating curveball in November 1995. Lying in bed next to Karen, I rolled over to kiss her goodnight, and she refused to kiss me.

"What's wrong?" I asked.

"I want a divorce."

"What? Is there someone else?"

"No."

"How serious is this?"

"I've hired an attorney. The sheriff will deliver the papers tomorrow at your office."

I felt my heart drop into my gut. I knew she wasn't happy, but a divorce had never entered my mind as a possibility. We'd just celebrated our eighteenth anniversary. Even though we were still struggling financially, I'd pulled some money together and bought her an expensive pearl necklace. I even wrote her a long letter telling her how much I loved her and that I knew I hadn't been the best husband over the past several years, but I wanted to be better and planned to work to be better.

"What can I do to make this work?"

"I need time and space to think."

"We can get through this."

"I want to keep the divorce moving forward. I think it's best if you find another place to live until we figure this out."

It was probably around midnight. I didn't want to stay next to her at that moment, so I packed some bags and left the house for a hotel.

Divorce is messy and painful, and it's amplified by a thousand when children are involved. I'm sharing this difficult episode of my personal journey because the experience was transformative and changed the trajectory of my life for the better. Because I hope to help others avoid the same mistakes I made, I will include some of the bad parts along with the good parts, not out of regret or to point fingers, but to show how life can and will throw you off course. By practicing resiliency, you can come out on the other side not only whole but better.

I felt blindsided by Karen asking for a divorce, but upon reflection over the years that followed, I know things hadn't been good between us for too long. Our marriage started to fail as the pizza business failed. Karen was handling all the household finances, while I dealt with business finances on my own. We weren't communicating during a time that demanded it the most.

When Karen asked for the divorce, I was working for Lozier on a salary of about $75,000 a year, but we were still over $100,000 in debt and had an expensive house payment on top of it all. My job put me on the road a lot, so whatever opportunity I had for effective spousal communication was diminished. When I was home, I just felt depressed. I shut down emotionally, gained weight, and wasn't involved with the family. I was never abusive physically or verbally, but emotionally, I had checked out. Karen did most of the family things with our daughters alone. I wasn't attending school events or kids sporting events. I didn't want to go to the dance recitals or theater events. If the kids had friends over, instead of playing games with them as I had in the past, I would disappear to another room.

Ultimately, we both made mistakes and broke promises to each other. I've learned relationships are fragile. They need constant nurturing and care, or they will die. That's the reality of the human condition. If you know something isn't working in your relationship with your significant other, you need to address it. The longer you put it off, the harder it becomes to reconcile. Once resentment sets in, it's almost impossible to overcome it.

I lost my wife of eighteen years, which broke my heart and shattered my world. But something emerged from that failure that changed me for the better. It's an outcome I never would have imagined could result in a happy ending: I became a single dad to two amazing young ladies, and the three of us would go through life as a three-person team for the next ten-plus years.

LIFE'S GREATEST REWARDS REVEAL THEMSELVES IN MYSTERIOUS WAYS

Life's greatest gifts can happen from events that start out as tragedies. They can transform you in ways you never imagined and lead to relationships that are rich with meaning and purpose. For reasons I won't get into here, I raised my daughters on my own from shortly after the divorce forward. The road to becoming a single dad not only cost me everything I owned, but it almost cost me my life.

One night before the girls lived with me full time, I tried taking my life. But I bailed out at the last second when I realized the most important thing to me was seeing my daughters grow up and knowing who they would become. To this day, I know I wouldn't be alive if it were not for Kelley and Lindsay.

When I started raising my girls as a single dad, they were ten and fourteen. Their mother was hurt and angry the girls chose to live with me. The result was she basically had little to nothing to do with the three of us for well over the next ten years. I had little clue what I was doing. I hadn't been as involved with their lives as I should've been over the past few years, and now I'd be acting as both parents full time. I didn't know what to do, so I did the only thing I could think of and had an open and honest conversation with them.

"I can't do this by myself," I said. "I can put groceries in the cupboard, but I can't make you eat. I can buy you books, but I can't make you study. I can give you guidance, but I can't make you choose right over wrong. There are people who think that living with a single dad will cause you to go astray in life. If you want to prove them right, you can. But if you want to prove those people wrong, then you need to do your part. I'll help you both in every possible way, but if you want us to be successful, we'll need to work as a team. I'm your father, and I love you, but I need your help."

Not only did my girls listen, but they understood what I was trying to communicate. I know it was a tough message for a ten- and fourteen-year-old to hear, but they lived up to it and then some. I gave them high expectations, told them I believed in them, but also let them know they had to be active participants in how their own story would later be told.

While work was important now that I was paying for everything on my own and starting over from scratch, I couldn't avoid being present in my girls' day-to-day lives. I needed to be at their school events, gym meets, plays, recitals, and other activities. No more being an absent father for me.

One of the greatest lessons I learned as a single dad was the importance of listening closely. It's not just with your children; it's really a life lesson for everyone you encounter. Parents, spouses, and friends often stop engaging after this question: "How are you doing?" You'll get a response like "I'm good," or "I'm fine," and the conversation is over. That's not a conversation. Nothing happened. No connection was made. You might as well have said nothing at all.

Some better questions I learned over the years:

"How are you feeling about our relationship?"

"How are you feeling about me?"

"What can I do more of to help you?"

"What can I do better?"

Those questions leave you vulnerable, but only through vulnerability can you connect in a meaningful way. And whatever you do, don't ask those questions unless you're ready for an honest answer. You might hear something that surprises you or hurts you. That's the point.

When my oldest daughter Kelley was fourteen, we had a conversation we still talk about to this day. Some events occurred between us that today I really don't recall. It doesn't matter, and most likely knowing her as I do, it was probably something minor that had become blown out of proportion by both of us. I just remember she was mad at me, and I was mad at her. If people who know me think I can sometimes be a bit stubborn, you should meet Kelley. Now add to her stubbornness being fourteen years old, and we have a tough situation.

We were going at it one evening, both of us frustrated and getting nowhere near a resolution, when I luckily landed on an epiphany. I'm guessing this may have been a moment of divine intervention! I remember saying, "Look, I'm trying. Honey, I've never been the dad to a fourteen-year-old daughter before, and you didn't come with an owner's manual. This is my first time. You need to help me as much as I help you, and maybe we need to cut each other a little slack."

That stopped the conflict. I dropped my stubbornness and went back to the honesty thing. I believe her hearing me admit I'm not perfect and that I wanted to work with her, not against her, was what allowed us to move forward and find a peaceful resolution.

Another lesson I learned was that our children's problems are just as big to them as our problems feel to us. We forget what it felt like to be a child. One day, for example, my younger daughter Lindsay was super stressed about an upcoming test. I remember thinking to myself, "You don't even know what stress is. I've got bills to pay, stacks of papers waiting for me on my desk, an intense meeting with the company owner tomorrow. You have no idea."

Thankfully, after I threw my pity party in my mind, I could see that her test was just as big a deal to her as my challenges the next day. Mine were not bigger or more important. In fact, I might have been feeling less stress because I was an adult. I had felt this way before and had tools to manage it. My daughter was still learning how to manage stress, so I sat down with her, talked with her about the art of test taking, and helped her prepare for her test. But the main thing I told her was we would not let a poor grade on some school test measure her. "Hell, Lindsay," I said, "I've flunked more tests than you or your sister ever will combined, and I'm doing okay. There's always another test and another day. Relax, do the best you can, and I love you no matter what grade you get."

That helped. She did fine on the test, and more importantly, she knew her dad had her back no matter what.

As a single dad, I was so worried they'd be like I was in high school. I remembered all the crap I did that my parents never had a clue about. Mom and Dad trusted me to do what's right, but I didn't. I was a thief and a drunk in high school, and my parents had no idea. I didn't want my daughters to make the same mistakes I did.

My worrying intensified after the girls got their driver's licenses. I worried less so about Kelley because of her intense gymnastics training—she never had time to find trouble. If I needed to find Kelley, all I had to do was go to the gym. But Lindsay was involved in everything and anything social. She was in cheerleading, choir, and theater. She had loads of friends. In her high school years, she would be "somewhere out" almost every night.

The nights I worried most were the ones when she told me she was going to "just hang out" with her friends. I remembered what that meant for me as a teenager. Sometimes I would drive around at night trying to find Lindsay's car at the local hot spots or at her friends' homes so I could ease my mind and stress. These were the days before cell phones and cell phone trackers, so it was common not to hear from her for much longer than I was comfortable with.

In the 1980s I became a big fan of President Ronald Reagan. I appreciated his phrase, "Trust but verify," which he recommended regarding treaties with the Soviet Union. I adopted this same philosophy with my teenage girls. I would "trust but verify."

If Lindsay told me she'd be at Liz's house, for example, I'd drive by Liz's house to see if her car was there. If she told me she would be at the bowling alley, I'd sneak inside and be very careful that she or her friends didn't see me. Occasionally, a day or two later, I might say something to her like, "Hey, at the bowling alley the other night, who was the tall boy with brown hair wearing the Nebraska T-shirt?"

She'd be incredulous. "You were in there? Were you spying on me?"

"Yeah," I'd say, "I stopped in but didn't want to bother you guys. Who was that boy?"

She'd tell me but then press me about why I had stopped by.

"Lindsay," I'd reply, "it's trust but verify. I trust you, but as your dad, I have a responsibility to verify once in a while. As long as you don't lie to me about where you're going or what you're doing, you have nothing to worry about."

Planting those seeds that I might verify occasionally was well worth the effort. Some people might say I went too far, but when you're a parent who is also playing the role of two parents without two sets of eyes on your children, you have to find ways to protect them.

In an earlier age of disconnected technology, that was my solution. My daughters didn't love it, but they knew I cared about them, and I think it's a hell of a lot more responsible than being an absent parent who doesn't care where their kids are at any given time.

I was fair to both girls and did a similar thing with Kelley one summer. My rule was neither of my daughters could drive their cars outside the city limits of Council Bluffs without my permission. The summer between Kelley's junior and senior years, she and her best friend Ashley decided they wanted to go to a country western bar in Omaha on teen night, so I called the establishment and made certain they did, in fact, have a teen night and what that meant. I found out it occurred once a month, no liquor was served, and it went until 2:00 a.m. No way was I letting Kelley be in West Omaha until 2:00 a.m. But after endless lobbying, I finally said yes, provided Kelley and Ashley gave me their word they would leave the establishment by no later than 11:00 p.m. I wanted them back on the Iowa side and home by midnight. Kelley didn't think it was the best deal but agreed to the terms.

Once again, I employed my trust but verify strategy. When they exited the bar at 11:00 p.m., they found me sitting on the hood of Kelley's car.

"Dad—what the hell? Don't you trust me?"

"Kelley, if I didn't trust you, I wouldn't have let you be here for one minute, let alone several hours. It's my job and my prerogative to verify that you keep your promise. Now here is twenty dollars. You and Ashley go to Taco Bell and get yourself something to eat. I'll see you at the house by midnight."

We've laughed about this little event many times since. I've had great satisfaction in seeing both Lindsay and Kelley use my same "trust but verify" techniques on their own children over the years.

I never thought I'd be a single dad, but it ended up being a wonderful gift. I'm blessed to have two amazing daughters who turned a tough situation into one of the things I cherish most in my life. One other very important outcome to this tragedy was I received another ball bat to the head, so to speak. When suddenly faced with being a single parent, I knew I had to improve in all aspects of my life, not just in parenting. It caused me to become more efficient at work, to take far better control of all of my finances, and to improve my time management. I truly believe this single event was the most significant cause of growth in my life. It made me a better dad, a better business person, and a better human.

It's also important to me to recognize the contribution of others in my journey as a single dad from 1995 forward. The assistance, moral support, and encouragement of some very close friends made a tremendous difference in my life. Had it not been for lifelong friends such as Jon and Kathy Wozniak, Marek Wozniak, Mark and Julia Doll, Greg and Buff Ross, Craig and Lori Whitney, and Brent and Val Siegrist offering their support, friendship, and encouragement, I would have had a far more difficult journey as a father. Through this ordeal, my parents also played an incredible role in helping me with the girls. When needed or if I was traveling for Lozier, they played taxi, chef, and backup whenever I asked.

MY BROTHER LARRY

As much business success as I was experiencing late in life, a lingering ache in my heart remained that no amount of real estate deals could heal. I'd done my best for forty years to sweep the emotional impact of my relationship with my brother Larry under the rug, but when you sweep things under the rug, they don't disappear. They remain where you put them. They live there in your house, and you have to step over them or look away and act like you don't see them.

Remember when I told you I was stubborn? Well, if you recall the vow I made sitting at Larry's graveside at his funeral, I told myself I would never step foot inside that cemetery again—and I didn't— for four decades. Then in 2010 I bought some land in our hometown.

Larry's gravesite was located only fifty feet off the road that I'd drive on every week as I went into town. If my mind wasn't occupied, I'd run the same recording in my brain every time I passed. "I'm not stopping, and I won't ever stop. I'm not stopping. I won't ever stop."

He was fifty feet away from the road, but I might as well have been 50,000 miles away. This routine repeated for ten years. Until I told a good friend about my fraught relationship with my brother, I realized I couldn't keep living like this. I was in pain; I was still angry, and the pain and anger weren't good for my mental or physical well-being. My friend suggested I talk with a therapist and try to work through the old wounds so I could stop thinking about it, so I followed her advice.

Jim, the therapist I worked with, ended up trying a technique called eye movement desensitization and reprocessing (EMDR), designed to alleviate the distress associated with traumatic memories and PTSD. I never thought of my relationship with Larry being so bad as to cause me post-traumatic stress disorder, but once I understood the markers, I ended up checking a lot of PTSD boxes.

I have to note that EMDR is a controversial topic in the psychology field, but it also seems that no one really knows what's going on in our brains, so how something becomes "controversial" too often seems tied to the special interests of those who profit off the latest whatever. My feeling is if it doesn't hurt you or anybody else, and it's useful, why the hell not try it? So I did.

EMDR relies on the Adaptive Information Processing (AIP) model, which is a theory about how your brain stores memories in a way that doesn't allow for healthy healing. Trauma lives in your mind like a wound your brain hasn't allowed to heal. Because the wound is not healed, your brain remains activated and reads the trauma as a threat, or like the danger is not over.

When you undergo EMDR, you combine eye movements with guided instructions from a therapist to access trauma in very specific ways. The technique enables you to get in touch with those memories and reprocess what you remember from negative events. That reprocessing helps "repair" the mental injury from that memory. The result is remembering what happened to you will no longer feel like you're reliving it, and the related feelings will be much more manageable.

Now that you know the clinical description of EMDR, let me give you the layperson's (Jerry's) description. The physical body has self-healing attributes we know and accept called white blood cells. They help the body fight infections and other diseases the best they can. Your subconscious also wants to self-heal, and it can recover from some traumas if allowed to do so. But occasionally, goofballs like me sweep things under rugs, blocking our mental self-healing mechanisms. EMDR works in most people who have lumps under their rugs, and it apparently does something I still can't figure out. Somehow, through some weird connection to eye movement, it cleans under the rug and allows the subconscious to heal and find peace. How and why it works with eye motion is beyond my pay grade. But, for me, EMDR worked, and in the end, that's all I need to know.

With that said, I thought doing EMDR was the goofiest damn thing I'd ever done in my life. It involved talking about my brother and focusing my eyes straight forward. While I told the story, the therapist made circles with his hand in front of my face as if going around the face of a clock. This movement continued throughout as I described my relationship with my brother.

After we finished one particular session, he asked, "At any point did my hand movement seem out of focus, blurry, or difficult?"

"Not really," I told him. "Maybe a little bit every time your hand got to about the eleven o'clock position, but that's probably due to my poor peripheral vision."

We talked about some other subjects for a bit. Then later he said, "Tell me the story of your brother again. I'm going to do the hand movement again in the clock circles with a slight change."

I told the story, but this time every time the therapist's hand hit the number eleven on the air clock, he seemed to use his fingers to throw something off the imaginary clock. Then he started his hand movement again, throwing something out at eleven o'clock throughout my storytelling. That was it! The session lasted about thirty minutes.

When we finished, I thought I'd completely wasted my time and that his goofy technique had no effect on me.

However, three weeks later on my way to town, as I approached the cemetery like I'd done countless times over the years, the negative avoidance recording in my head did not start. Instead, I pulled into the cemetery. The next thing I knew, I was standing over my brother's grave marker for the first time since the day he was laid to rest.

Standing there, I saw a flat slab memorial I'd never seen before because my parents had added it after Larry's funeral. My brother's hobby in life was flying, and he had a small plane he flew often. The flat slab was engraved with a 1941 poem by Pilot Officer John Gillespie Magee Jr. titled "High Flight."

HIGH FLIGHT

Oh! I have slipped the surly bonds of Earth
And danced the skies on laughter-silvered wings;
Sunward I've climbed, and joined the tumbling mirth
Of sun-split clouds—and done a hundred things
You have not dreamed of—wheeled and soared and swung
High in the sunlit silence. Hov'ring there,
I've chased the shouting wind along, and flung
My eager craft through footless halls of air.

Up, up the long, delirious, burning blue
I've topped the wind-swept heights with easy grace
Where never lark nor ever eagle flew—
And, while with silent lifting mind I've trod
The high untrespassed sanctity of space,
Put out my hand, and touched the face of God.[5]

---

[5] John Gillespie Magee Jr., "High Flight," Poetry Foundation, https://www.poetryfoundation.org/poems/157986/high-flight-627d3cfb1e9b7.

I didn't really feel any strong emotions while reading the poem or after I finished. I was in the moment. It was different than I imagined it would be. I didn't feel anger like I thought I might. If anything, I felt a calmness. I'd begun allowing myself to release my anger and do something I hadn't done in forty years: grieve for the loss of my brother.

Three months later, I was doing some real estate consulting for a gentleman in the area. He asked me to fly with him to Greenville, Texas, on his private jet. It was raining hard that day, but we had a safe flight and landed at the tiny airport in Greenville. We made our way off the plane and hustled out of the rain and into the small operations building off the runway.

As I walked toward the building, my mind was consumed with the property I was commissioned to evaluate, but God had something else in store for me at that small-town Texas airport. After I entered the building, something on the wall caught my eye. Walking closer to examine it, I couldn't believe what I was seeing: a large, hand-painted artist's version of the "High Flight" poem I had seen for the first time at Larry's gravesite three months earlier.

I lost all sense of where I was.

I felt as though I was alone inside a dense fog having an out-of-body experience, as much as such a thing exists. In my heart, I felt someone talking to me—maybe Larry, maybe God, or maybe some unnamed angel. I heard voices talking and repeating clearly the words, "It's okay. Let it go. It's okay. Let it go. Let it go. Let it go."

Suddenly, a feeling of peace washed over me. That divine moment filled the hole in my heart I'd been living with for four decades. I felt a tap on my shoulder from my client and close friend Denny that brought me out of the moment.

"Jerry, are you okay?"

Recovering my senses, I told him the story of the poem and its relationship to my brother's grave. Denny put his hands on my shoulders, looked me in the eye, and said, "Jerry, I get it—take your time."

As we left, Denny said, "Jerry, take a picture of that wall, and remember this moment."

The pain and anger were no longer under the rug. I had pulled the rug up, faced my anguish, and found out I'd be okay. I didn't have to feel this way anymore.

You can call this amazing experience whatever you want: a God moment, a message from an angel, or an unexpected spiritual event. I don't know. I just know it changed my world. For years I had buried feelings of anger that were amplified by never being able to talk it out. Why did Larry help persuade me to go to Vietnam? Did he even care about my safety? Why had he been so verbally abusive to me all my life?

The worst part about my estranged relationship with Larry was never having the opportunity to find out if my brother and I could've reconciled and been friends as adults. Would we have gotten along? Would our feelings have been different? In answer to these nagging questions, I remembered two pieces of advice. This first one: "Forgiveness is a gift you give yourself." I'd known that for years, and I'd quoted it to many people, but in relation to my brother, I hadn't applied it. Some of us are great at giving lessons and lectures to others but don't always apply them to our own lives consistently. I can be a hypocrite. I think we all are at times. With my relationship to my brother and his untimely death, I was unwilling to address my own hypocrisy about the gift of forgiveness.

The other piece of advice by self-help author Robert Brault came into my life a couple of years after the Greenville event, but I've thought about it extensively since: "Life becomes easier when you learn to accept the apology you never got." No question, my life got easier that day in Greenville, Texas. I finally accepted an apology I never received but had wanted for over forty years. After this series of events, I could also finally think about forgiving my brother. I realized I couldn't go back and change anything. I wondered what Larry's experience in life was to cause him to say and do the things he did and said to me. I'd also grown and learned enough to understand that my brother likely had baggage he was dealing with that he sometimes unloaded on me.

Best of all, I remembered a sweet moment we shared that I hadn't thought about maybe since the time it happened. When I was four years old, my parents went out to dinner a few nights before Christmas. They left my eleven-year-old brother in charge. I know, different times back then.

We decided to gently unwrap our presents. Larry showed me how to undo one end so no one could tell, then slide the gift out. We scouted out all our gifts and were in the process of rewrapping them when we spotted car headlights in the driveway. Larry told me to go to bed and pretend I was asleep. He hid the evidence under the backside of the tree. After Mom and Dad went to bed, he went back to the living room and finished rewrapping the remaining gifts. No one knew the difference, and it was years before we told Mom and Dad about it.

Larry had my back like a big brother should that night. It's a little thing in retrospect, but it's the little things that define our relationships, and it's a memory I'm thankful came back to me—one I'll never forget.

In the last four years, I've been even more mindful of the benefits of siblings and wished I would have had one or more. As it became necessary to move my parents into an independent living facility, then later to assisted living, and then to experience the process of hospice and death for both of them, the benefit of a sibling to share the experience with sure would have been nice. My daughters helped enormously and had to fill the shoes of being granddaughters, daughters, and, to a degree, substitute siblings in trying to advise and assist me through this journey.

I still get emotional about some of those hard memories with my brother. I still hurt at times. I still wish I'd had a normal (whatever the hell normal is) relationship with my sibling. But I've finally accepted the past for what it is, and most importantly, I've found peace through forgiveness.

My best advice to any of my readers is to give gratitude to your siblings and loved ones in life. I'm sure they aren't perfect, but hopefully, they're still in your life. I had no warnings that on August 7, 1976, my brother would be taken, and we would never again have the chance to talk. If you're not on good terms with one of your siblings (or any other loved one), do everything you can to make it right. You never know when life will take them from you, and your opportunity to make peace in this life will be gone forever.

YOUR GPS INPUT CHECKLIST

- Tragedy can be a catalyst for personal growth and transformation, leading to unexpected blessings.
- Listening attentively and empathetically to others, especially your children, is critical for building strong bonds.
- The art of "trust and verify" can be a valuable approach in parenting, ensuring safety and accountability.
- Forgiveness is a powerful act of self-healing that can liberate you from the pain of the past and open the door to inner peace.
- Cherish and nurture your relationships with loved ones because the opportunity for reconciliation can be taken away from you without notice.

CHAPTER 10

GENERATING MAXIMUM HAPPINESS

"You can have everything in life you want,
if you will just help enough other people get what they want."

—Zig Ziglar

Remember my happiness chart from the introduction to this book? Now you have a better sense of what I was talking about. Life, and the happiness I've experienced throughout it, is a roller coaster.

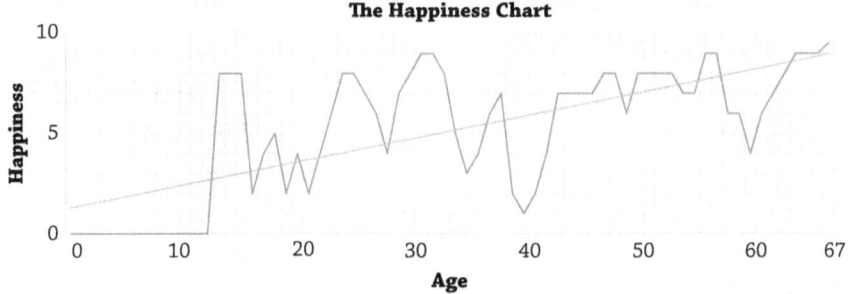

Keep in mind that I also warned that happiness can be fleeting, and you need to find joy in the process of living. That's true for both the ups and downs life throws at you. You can't manipulate your ride to be nothing but a smooth ascending ride of joy, but I believe you can learn to better handle and survive your low points by programming your internal GPS system with the 4 Ds +1.

The first D, dreaming, is foundational. Remember, the only rule about dreaming is you must believe in your dreams to have a shot at achieving them. Your dreams set your course, give you something to aim for, and will most likely change along your journey. You saw how many times mine did.

The second D, decisions, are the choices you make along your journey. You'll confront countless decisions, and although you won't always make the right ones, what's most important is making a decision. If you're wrong, note what happened, learn from it, and redirect your course. Remember, one way to make better decisions is by asking yourself, "Is this decision in alignment with my dream?"

The third D, determination, relates to your will to move forward when life gets tough. Think of determination as mile markers on your progress highway. Sometimes you have to keep your head down and do your best to make it to the next mile marker. When the detours and roadblocks interrupt your path, it's your ability to stay determined and keep going that will get you back on the right path. Detours are temporary by definition.

The fourth D, discipline, is your mental ability to follow through with actions that support your dreams and goals. Often with discipline, there are no external roadblocks or detours impeding your path—the obstacle is in your head. Will you do what you know you need to do, or will you let distractions keep you from making progress? Will you put in an hour of reading time each night so you can learn the skills you need to achieve your goals, or will you turn on the TV? Will you do good work or excellent work? Discipline can separate you from your competitors if you're disciplined to go beyond good to excellence.

The plus one, resiliency, is your ability to adjust or recover from adversity. Your ability to bounce back from hard times is the most important factor in achieving your dreams. You can get the 4 Ds right, but when tragedy launches you off the road and into a ditch, only resiliency can save you.

Life is not fair. You've heard this line countless times throughout your life. But it's like saying the sky is blue. So what? It's not helpful. What is useful is somebody saying life is not fair, so here are some tools you can use to get through it to help you create the best life possible despite the unfairness.

Whether we like it or not, most of us have two options when life slings a pile of shit in our face. We can give up, or we can eat shit and smile. I don't know why we have to eat so much shit, but that's how life is for most people. That's how it has been for me. Again, this is not a new story. It's just a different way to understand it, and hopefully a way that helps you.

Remember: Happiness and success don't require greatness. If you're striving for perfection and greatness, you're putting way too much unrealistic pressure on yourself. In the long run, being perfect will hamper you. Happiness and success come from an understanding of the levers you must pull and the tools you must use to create a fulfilling life for yourself. If you've made it this far, you have a new set of tools to help you generate maximum happiness. Use these tools when things are going your way, use them when tragedy strikes, but above all—use them.

SUCCESS ISN'T EVERYTHING

An interesting discovery you'll make on your journey is when you reach a significant destination and fulfill a dream, a whole new section of the map opens up. Previously, your focus on a specific destination prevented you from seeing another dream beyond your first one. The possibility of a new dream may never have occurred to you, but once you see it, it's impossible to ignore, and you get to start a new adventure.

For me, discovering new dreams has become an addiction and the highlight of my journey. It took over twenty-three years of working at Lozier before I realized it was time to embark on something new. The difficult decision to leave Lozier took me around three years from initially considering it until my last day at the office. Despite earning a tremendous salary and holding a prestigious title, I was unhappy. My job required me to travel about 125 days a year, and my relationship with my boss became strained. My personal life was in turmoil, as a subsequent marriage was failing. Many days I didn't want to go to work, and I didn't want to go home. I knew something had to change.

In January 2016 I told Allan I was ready to transition out of the company. It took him a few days to realize I was serious. We'd reached a point where it'd be in our mutual best interest to change leadership at NewStreet Properties. My heart wasn't in it to the degree he deserved, and I think his patience with me was growing thin.

Negotiations on my departure and the buyout of my partnership share ran from the end of January through March. We closed on my buyout in May. Allan asked me to help find my replacement. I made a short list of individuals I thought would be potential candidates. Brian Diedrichsen came to mind. I'd worked with Brian in the acquisition of a significant Omaha apartment complex a few years earlier. I found him sharp, even keeled, and excellent to work with. After reviewing his bio, I realized he had the credentials and background to make the cut.

So I reached out to Brian. We met, and I downloaded to him the good, the bad, and the ugly of my position over twenty-three-plus years. He called the next day and said he wanted to apply for the position. Within a few weeks, Lozier hired him, and he remains at the helm of NewStreet to this day. I stayed on salary and assisted with the transition until September. I'm so blessed and proud to say that on my last day, I shook hands with Allan, said my goodbyes, and walked out the front door versus being thrown out the back door.

During the transition period, I took serious stock of my life and asked myself some tough questions. I wrote a letter to myself, asking what I wanted my life to be about over the next ten to twenty years, breaking it down into three major categories: career, family, and Jerry.

For my career, I determined I wanted to use my brain, energy, time, and finances to make a positive difference in the world. I planned to accomplish this by using my skill sets to provide safe places for people to live and work, improve communities through good design, help others on my team learn and grow, and donate my time and money to causes I'm passionate about.

I centered my family goals around the desire to become a catalyst to help my loved ones become contributing members of society, excel at their endeavors, live with humility and respect for others, expand their world, prepare for the future, and achieve their dreams. At this point, I had five grandkids (now seven!), and I wanted to spend more time with them. Also, both my parents were aging. Mom was eighty-eight, and Dad was ninety-five. I wanted to spend more time with them.

The third component I focused on was myself. I aimed to meet and spend time with interesting people, surround myself with positivity, and improve myself mentally, physically, and spiritually to create more happiness in my life.

After laying out these three areas, I asked myself a crucial question: How do I achieve my purpose? To make things happen, I knew I needed to program the right information into my internal GPS system to reach my destinations. I considered inputs related to people, time, and resources. Before deciding, I developed a new habit of questioning how each person I interacted with, each project I undertook, each investment I made, and each time commitment I accepted or action I took contributed to my three primary priorities. If I couldn't directly correlate my actions, time, investments, and commitments to one of my three priorities, I couldn't do it.

I had good inputs, but I didn't want to merely dream and take the long way. I wanted to make it happen as soon as I could, so I committed to acting every day to promote or advance at least one of my three priorities. For example, I started scheduling trips with my family. My dad had always wanted to visit Alaska, but my mom hated to travel. I knew if I told Mom I'd go along, she would give in. I also wrangled

Lindsay and her daughter Evie to come with us. In the fall of 2016, I took my parents at ages ninety-five and eighty-eight, along with Lindsay and Evie, on an Alaskan cruise. It wasn't an easy trip, as my parents had a hard time because of their ages, but making one of my dad's dreams come true was gratifying.

Perhaps the most crucial input I entered into my internal GPS was to think big. This meant rejecting the easy way, pushing myself to achieve more by being unique and stepping outside the box. I didn't want to be a lemming, blindly following others off a cliff. I knew the last thing I wanted to do was to retire. Hit the reset button—yes. Retire? Never!

To help ensure I'd meet my new goals, I retained a life coach: Lori Stohs of Lori Stohs Consulting Group. Lori has ample experience coaching people who are transitioning in their careers. She was a significant help and remains both a friend and adviser to this day. One of the most impactful tools she shared with me was the "I want—I Don't Want" Matrix. Before I could look at any new opportunities, Lori had me do the matrix exercise in which I listed four major categories to measure each opportunity I examined.

The matrix looks like this:

	What I want	What I don't want
My Role		
Company		
Leader or Boss		
Team		

Prior to working with Lori, I was good at concentrating on what I wanted. It was part of my GPS programming. What I hadn't done a good job of was examining what I didn't want.

After leaving Lozier, I put the matrix to work when I was approached with the idea of working for a significant family-owned real estate company in Omaha. After measuring this new opportunity against the matrix, I quickly realized it wasn't a good fit. They were good people, but I knew my happiness was not down that path, and I politely excused myself from consideration.

A few months after that opportunity knocked on my door, a second one came knocking. I received a call one day from Ken Cook, the CEO of East Campus Realty. East Campus Realty was the development arm of Mutual of Omaha, and Ken was serving on a voluntary board associated with the University of Nebraska Medical Center (UNMC). Ken asked if I'd be interested in doing consulting work for the UNMC. Interestingly enough, Ken and I went to high school together in Glenwood, Iowa. After several meetings with Ken and administrators at UNMC, and after measuring the opportunity against my "I Want—I Don't Want" Matrix, I agreed to a part-time consulting assignment to help UNMC expand their campus by acquiring properties and developing the west side of Saddle Creek Road in Omaha.

Over the next four years I helped acquire several properties, both on the west and east side of Saddle Creek Road. The new campus expansions are under construction today and will involve hundreds of millions of dollars in new investments. The people whom I worked with at UNMC, along with their selected developers, were visionaries and incredibly smart. Everyone had a singular vision to create something significant, workable, and that we could all be proud of fifty to one hundred years down the road.

Today, as I drive by the area and see what's under construction, I take a great amount of pride in being able to tell my grandkids that I played a small role in making it happen. A secondary benefit has been making friends with some folks we acquired property from. I had a great experience that fit my priorities using my brain, energy, and time to serve my goals of making the world a better place.

I encourage you to try incorporating the "I Want—I Don't Want" Matrix into your decision-making and see what happens. I think you'll be surprised how it forces you to get clarity on the full picture before moving forward on a decision.

WHY ISN'T FINANCIAL SUCCESS EVERYTHING?

Achieving success and reaching major milestones in your industry by becoming a powerful person with status, especially in business or your career, can seem like the most important thing in life because getting to the top takes a lot of hard work. It can take years or decades. But here's the problem: Most of the people who make it are very motivated individuals, and when they get there, they discover there's more to life than money, power, and status.

Personally, I never set a goal of money or power. My main goal was always to be the best at whatever I was doing. If it was owning Century 21, then I wanted the number one market share. At Lozier, I wanted to build a large, successful portfolio that stood the test of time. My dreams were never about money or power. When I reflect on my life up to this point, and all the difficulties I've faced along the way, most of the time I was pursuing whatever I believed success for me would be at the time, but when I achieved it, I realized there was more to life, and reaching that point was part of the journey; it wasn't everything.

I've realized that what I've overcome in life means far more to me personally than any achievements I was fortunate enough to garner. Knowing that I was able to overcome and survive the roller coaster lows has been far more personally satisfying to me than anything else.

When you achieve whatever success looks like to you, you witness new possibilities you couldn't imagine before. As I said, the map expands, and new lands appear. But here's the catch: You need to have the resources that come from business and career success to explore those new lands. It's a realistic matter. It's hard to make a difference when you're barely making ends meet, so no matter where you are in your journey, remember that as you keep advancing toward your goal, there will be a moment when you get there, and the map will reveal things to you that you never dreamed before.

ENJOY THE RIDE

I came across a quote that people mistakenly attribute to Abraham Lincoln, but it reminds me of what Mr. Colwell told me in that café when I was beginning my career in real estate: "Business brings problems as surely as planting potatoes brings bugs. The person with spirit attacks the bugs. They don't stop planting potatoes." That means you don't quit just because you face a lot of difficult shit in your life. You need to stay positive, keep working, and fight the bugs with a smile on your face!

My challenges early in my career were not only real estate and not only bugs in the potatoes. Everything was a challenge! I finally realized the people who can cope and handle problems while still helping other people are extraordinary. If you can help solve other people's problems while managing your own, you will prosper. Solving problems and taking responsibility are two indicators of people who achieve success. A company doesn't want to advance somebody who can't handle or solve problems. They want people who thrive on responsibility. Those individuals are the ones who earn the promotions.

Along my journey, I learned obstacles and failures are my treasure. They're my chance to excel. I didn't always understand that, but as I remained determined and kept working on the problem, the situation changed from being a problem to an amazing opportunity.

Obviously I still face challenges. I'll always encounter new challenges. Today my first response to a new problem is, "How can I deal with this?" Now I have a method. I pause and think about the challenge at hand. Then I plan ways to overcome each new challenge and turn the challenge into an opportunity. Part of my mentoring involves helping my colleagues see challenges as opportunities. That's a big change in perspective. I tell them my stories of overcoming adversity and show them the tools I used to not only get through the hard times, but to make them work in my favor.

Life is a roller coaster. It has highs and lows. So does a day, so does a week, so does a year. When the coaster is plunging in a downward spiral, I hold on, knowing I'll go up again soon enough. And when you're on top, it's important to remember the lows are coming. You can't avoid them, but you can be mindful and do your best to prepare. Knowing you'll get through the lows and enjoy the highs makes life a more manageable experience. Do your best to find joy in the process, regardless of the ups or downs.

GIVING BACK IS THE GREATEST GIFT

I always remember the hard times and how they affected me. I appreciate having people who supported and trusted me. The best way for me to thank them is to do the same for others: help them and give them generosity, wisdom, and guidance.

Allan Lozier taught me so much about life. He told me once that the day you were born in America, you won the lottery. The day you were born to a Midwestern white family, you were blessed. And the day you were born a male, you had advantages. My silent reaction was, "What are you talking about? You're crazy. How could being born a male give me an advantage?"

As the years went by and I opened my eyes to the surrounding reality, I saw his point. I started thinking about my mom and what she went through. I recognized the fact that women weren't supposed to talk about their problems in her era. While raising two daughters,

I witnessed many instances where people treated them differently from boys—and often inappropriately. They weren't supposed to do what boys did. They rarely received the same recognition for their achievements as their male classmates. If you wanted to raise money for sports, it was a one-way street, but if it was a boy's sport, there was a big budget available. If you needed equipment or money for football or boys' basketball, it was there in abundance, but if you needed supplies or equipment for theater, arts, or girls' sports, it was second-hand-me-down crap. Those experiences got my attention.

Dianne Lozier, Allan's wife, was heavily involved in women's issues, and we discussed the disparity more than once. Thankfully, her heart for women's advancement won me over as I listened and learned. Some people refer to it as advancing women's rights, but I believe it encompasses much more. Borrowing something Allan said, I dream of helping to level the playing field during this phase of my journey. I cannot cure everything in the world, America, or even my home states of Iowa or Nebraska, but I can try to make a difference in my hometown.

Helen Keller had a perfect quote that describes how I feel about giving: "I cannot do everything, but still I can do something; and because I cannot do everything, I will not refuse to do something that I can do."[6]

Over the years, I met others with similar passion, and together we founded the Women's Fund of Southwest Iowa, which covers seven counties in Iowa. To help kick it off, I put my money where my mouth was. Our wonderful team of volunteers invests the funds in organizations throughout the seven counties surrounding Glenwood and Council Bluffs to help level the playing field for girls and women. Our initiatives include promoting STEM curriculum educational programs for girls, investing in lower-cost daycare options for single mothers who must work to support their families, and helping teenage moms

---

[6] Helen Keller, "I Cannot Do Everything," *The Book of Good Cheer: A Little Bundle of Cheery Thoughts*, ed. Edwin Osgood Grover (P.F. Volland Co., 1909), 28.

who struggle to complete their education while taking care of their children. Even small gestures, such as providing transportation to and from school for a single teen mom, can be a big help.

At the other end of the spectrum, elderly females live far longer than their male counterparts. Most of the males from that generation were the higher wage earners. When the higher wage earner dies first, too often the partner left behind has a far lower Social Security income. If they don't have enough income, they may be forced to sell their home or move. Add the pressure of more medical bills, and it can become overwhelming. We seek ways through nonprofit organizations to help fund staying in place for elderly women whenever possible.

Sex trafficking is another huge problem, and our organization also aims to build awareness and confront those issues. Today I'm proud to say I'm the only male on the Women's Fund of Southwest Iowa Steering Committee. I can't solve all the problems in the world, America, or even my local community, but I try my best to make some sort of difference.

Another way that I give is through collecting contemporary art. There's a special story behind that. My two daughters both have unique talents. My older daughter Kelley was an outstanding athlete, and now she's one of the best elite gymnastics coaches for girls in the country. She won many gymnastic medals and trophies when she was young, and she earned a gymnastics scholarship to George Washington University. While Kelley was getting all those awards, my youngest daughter Lindsay had a hard time with her self-image in her early years.

Lindsay didn't win trophies and medals in sports like her sister, but then almost accidentally, she discovered live theater. Or maybe I should say live theater found her. From about age five through high school, Lindsay performed numerous speaking and singing roles live in community and school theater. She was active in choir and performance choir, and often sang the National Anthem at her high school events. She won awards in high school for her performances, appeared in television commercials, and acted in a twenty-minute movie produced by the Nebraska Game and Parks Commission. She built her self-confidence through the arts and literally found her voice. Your passion doesn't have to be sports or academics. Art can help our youth find their confidence and expression. Both performance art and aesthetic arts are wonderful for our youth.

As a result of my learning about what the arts can accomplish, and my love for contemporary art, I served for fifteen years on the board of directors of the Bemis Center for Contemporary Arts in Omaha and today serve on their strategic planning committee. Through my participation in this world-class organization, I not only felt I was giving back, but I also met some amazing people and witnessed firsthand the growth and achievement of several artists.

As I've discussed throughout this book, balance in work, life, family, emotions, and more are all important. I hope you find the time to give back to your community, causes that matter to you, and to other people in your life. Giving back is not just about networking (which is important), but it's rewarding to your soul to know that in some small way you make a positive difference. That can involve donating money to a cause or offering your help. I think karma is real, and what you give to the world will return to you. You can either take or give. Be a giver as much as you can.

I have a special karma trick I've used for years. If I feel like I'm in a streak of bad luck, and everything is going against me in the world, I have a cure for it. I start writing checks to my favorite nonprofits, or I increase my volunteer time and efforts. I view it as a karma thing. When karma is working against me, I fix it by giving and turn my karma around to a positive. It's worked for me every time.

A saying I like that sometimes gets attributed to Winston Churchill goes like this: "We make a living by what we get, but we make a life by what we give." I urge you to give because as you give, you will realize the true meaning and worth of the quote, and it will help you make a wonderful life for you and your family.

In his series of books *Meditations*, Roman Emperor Marcus Aurelius wrote, "When you arise in the morning, think of what a precious privilege it is to be alive—to breathe, to think, to enjoy, to love!"[7] That's where I've landed on my roller coaster journey. Every morning, I recognize what a privilege it is to breathe, think, enjoy, and love! I hope this book will help you on your own journey and encourage you to not give up when your world seems like it's crashing in on you. As Coach Jim Valvano said in his famous speech at the 1993 ESPY Awards, "Never give up. Don't ever give up."[8]

I'd like to end by expressing my greatest wish for you: You will dream; you will make decisions that take you in the direction of your dreams; you will be determined; and you will be disciplined. But mostly, you will be resilient enough to eat shit and smile!

---

[7] Marcus Aurelius, *Meditations*, trans. Gregory Hays (Modern Library, 2002), 17.

[8] Jim Valvano, "Jim's 1993 ESPY Speech," ESPY Awards, March 4, 1993, https://www.youtube.com/watch?v=HuoVM9nm42E.

ACKNOWLEDGMENTS

Where do I start? Listing people is dangerous because I fear leaving someone out whom I will remember after publication and regret it. So, to all those I fail to mention specifically, please know it was unintentional. I have already mentioned a lot of people by name throughout the book, so I won't repeat those names here.

To all my teachers at Glenwood Community Schools through my twelve years of attendance, let me first apologize. I should have done better. Thank you for tolerating me. To my classmates of the graduating class of 1973 (and surrounding years), thank you for the fun times, friendship, help in hiding our misdeeds, and remaining friends as a close-knit group to this day. The older I get, the more I appreciate all of you and our enduring friendship.

To the people of Glenwood, Iowa. Growing up in Glenwood, I have often said, was like growing up in Mayberry R.F.D. I cherish the memories along my journey. Glenwood is an amazing place. I fully recognize that the people and culture who were present in my youth played a significant and positive role in my life. Thank you.

To my attorney and friend Gary Gotsdiner and his associate Keith Green, we first started working together in the late 1980s or the days of Breadeaux Pizza. You have not only been great advocates and advisers through billions of dollars of transactions, but you have also held my hand and advised me through the dips in that roller coaster of life. Both in the dips and the peaks, you were there for me and my family. My gratitude is beyond explanation.

To the folks of NewStreet Properties/Lozier, I cannot express to you enough my deep appreciation for your hard work, professionalism, friendship, and guidance through my twenty-three-plus years. I know I will miss someone, but I want to specifically call out Sheri, Bob, Jan, Tre, Barb, Trayce, Henri, Kristi, Ginny, Lisa, Ben, and Patrick. You all played a significant role in my NewStreet/Lozier journey. Our track record from starting with nothing to what NewStreet has become is a testament to each of you. Thank you for always having my backside, and thank you for your friendship.

To Rachel Rodenburg, my Family Office Controller, your official title is way too limited. You are my internal accountant, my administrative assistant, my friend and more. Rachel, thank you so much for making my life easier and better. You make me look good and you put up with and cover for my absent-minded tendencies. I couldn't do what I do without your help. You have my respect and appreciation. Thank you!

To Dave Burchett, my friend and husband of my cousin Joni, your guidance, assistance, push, and belief in me made this book possible and better from beginning to end. Thank you!

To the fine folks of Peacock Proud Press and their affiliated team—Laura, James, Jena, and Erin. You took an idea and made it a reality. I will forever remember your push, professionalism, encouragement, and patience.

To my friend Cindy, your friendship, help, guidance, encouragement, and ear has always and will *always* mean the world to me.

To my parents, there is no way I can honor you properly for your love, guidance, example, and contributions to my life. May you both rest in peace. I love you.

To my daughters, trying to express to you how much I love you and how much I credit you for my journey and survival is nearly impossible. We have been through hell together and survived. We have traveled the world together and experienced some amazing times. Whenever I reached the bottom side of life's roller coaster, all I've had to do was be with you, or think of you, and I knew I had to do better—that life would get better. Whenever I wanted to celebrate the rewards of life, I wanted it to be with you. You have been my inspiration, my advisers, my critics, my shoulder to lean on, my push from behind. And then, as a bonus, you rewarded me with two wonderful sons-in-law, Mike and Darren, and seven grandkids, who are my pride, my joy, my fun, and even more reason to stay the course.

To my grandkids, there isn't a day that goes by that I don't think of each of you. You have brought so much joy, happiness, laughter, and love to my life that I never imagined possible. I can't wait to watch and cheer your journey. I unconditionally love you, now and forever.

ABOUT THE AUTHOR

Jerry G. Banks is the Principal and Founder of Jerry Banks Group, headquartered in Omaha, Nebraska. With a career that spans decades, Jerry has managed $2 billion in real estate transactions, including apartments, retail spaces, warehouses, and development properties across the United States. He also leads JBG Services, Inc., offering real estate consulting to clients like the University of Nebraska, Mutual of Omaha, and several high-net-worth families.

Prior to founding Jerry Banks Group in 2016, Jerry was a partner in NewStreet Properties, LLC, where he managed over $1.5 billion in transactions, including 8,000 apartment units and 2 million square feet of industrial property. He was inducted into the Nebraska Commercial Real Estate Hall of Fame in 2016.

Jerry's entrepreneurial ventures extend beyond real estate. He has owned thirteen pizza franchises, a residential real estate company, a bar, an advertising agency, and a small property management firm. He knows the grit and grind it takes to build a small business.

A proud single father and grandfather, Jerry raised two daughters and relishes spending time with his seven grandchildren. He enjoys the outdoors, art projects, ATV's, hiking, collecting contemporary art, travelling, and spending time with family and friends at his second home in Scottsdale, Arizona.

Jerry gives back by serving on numerous boards, including on the Board of Trustees for Dakota REIT, the Real Estate Strategic Planning Committee of the Bemis Center for Contemporary Art, and the Steering Committee of the SW Iowa Women's Fund. Historically Jerry served as a volunteer on several nonprofit boards in both Iowa and Nebraska.

Now a mentor, speaker, and author, Jerry shares his knowledge and experiences in *Eat Sh*t & Smile* to show readers how to navigate the ups and downs of life using his unique Internal GPS System. Jerry helps others achieve peace, happiness, and success with greater ease than he did.

Want Jerry to speak to your organization?
Visit his website
jerrygbanks.com

Follow Jerry on LinkedIn
linkedin.com/in/jerrygbanks/